HUMP DAY DEVOTIONALS

Introduction:

My name is Jackson Bailey. I am a comedian, teacher, preacher, author, coach, husband, dad, and Christ-Follower (but not in that particular order). I have a beautiful wife and two wonderful children. I'm thankful for the family God has blessed me with, and I love family time! Family devotion time is one of my favorites, but sometimes it can begin to feel like we're forcing ourselves to do it. One day we changed things up. We shared some stories about our lives and talked about how we could apply Scripture to them. The next night we acted out the Bible story. We began to change things up on a regular basis to keep it creative, fresh and new. The Bible IS creative, fresh and new all the time. But we, as humans, tend to get bogged down and need to remind ourselves that what we're reading is true and exciting!

I love family devotional time, and I love stories. Now admittedly we are a strange family. Even for my family I've always been a bit unusual, and maybe that's why my life has been filled with interesting things that have happened to me. I also come from a long line of family members that are great storytellers. I'm far from the best storyteller in my family, but, alas, I do have a lot of stories to tell. I've always wanted to get some of these stories on paper. As I was working one day, I felt led to write a devotional book that was full of my personal stories that have helped me learn important life lessons. Every Wednesday for a year I wrote a devotional, and so I called them "Hump Day Devotionals."

Everyone struggles with the frustrations of this life, and it seems we begin to feel like we're all alone. Rest assured, YOU ARE NOT ALONE! God taught me so much through the writing of this book. My prayer is that He will use it to help you grow, and think about Him. When riding a bicycle you sometimes look ahead and see a hill coming. So you attempt to create enough speed going downhill to help you get over that hump that is ahead. You use that momentum, and then as that momentum begins to die, you peddle. And the bigger the hill, the harder you have to peddle. Think of these little stories as your momentum, and the Scriptures can be your peddles. Sometimes we just need a little truth to help us get over the hump, right? Ya know? Like a spiritual double shot of Godly espresso! Here are 52 "Hump Day Devotionals" to help you get over that hump. I know I've titled the book "Hump Day Devotionals," but you don't have to read it on Wednesday or with a camel! Try reading it on Monday and meditating on the scriptures for the rest of the week. Maybe you can share the story and the lesson with your coworkers and friends, or use it as a conversation starter. It would be awesome to use it as an after-dinner devotion with your family. If nothing else make it your "bathroom book." Maybe you can start a Bible study with it or give it away to anyone and everyone you meet. Whatever and however you may use it, my prayer is that it will be a blessing to you and that it will honor Jesus Christ our Lord and Savior. Get on your spiritual bicycle and start peddling with 52 WEEKS OF HUMP DAY DEVOTIONALS!

WEEK 1

Get Over the Hump Day A NEW YEAR RESOLUTION Devotional:

Throughout the years I have resolved to do many things. Work out my abs until I finally get a six pack, read my Bible every day, treat others the way I want to be treated, give more, live more, do more... and make a million dollars so I can give more, live more, and do more. I start out doing really well, but by about February 1st, I've lost it. I know that's sad, but true. I have reached certain goals: I got close to a four pack just above my muffin top, I read my Bible a lot, I treated others the way I wanted to be treated.... (occasionally), and I made enough money to eat and provide for my family (Praise God). But I fell really, really, really short of that million. I'm still trying to make resolutions and better myself, and I hope I keep doing that until I die. And I hope you do too. Here's what I want to say to you: DON'T GIVE UP. DON'T STOP. Sins in your life will always need to be defeated, and people will always need your influence. You must finish the race.

<u>2 Timothy 4:3-8</u>

3 For the time is coming when people will not endure sound teaching, but having itching ears they will accumulate for themselves teachers to suit their own passions, 4 and will turn

away from listening to the truth and wander off into myths. 5 As for you, always be sober-minded, endure suffering, do the work of an evangelist, fulfill your ministry.
6 For I am already being poured out as a drink offering, and the time of my departure has come. 7 I HAVE FOUGHT THE GOOD FIGHT, I HAVE FINISHED THE RACE, I HAVE KEPT THE FAITH. 8 Henceforth there is laid up for me the crown of righteousness, which the Lord, the righteous judge, will award to me on that Day, and not only to me but also to all who have loved his appearing.

That time is here. People are not enduring sound teaching. They are following people who tell them what they want to hear, even though the Bible clearly states differently. Your faith will be tested. Be ready. Fight and Finish. Don't give up. Jesus went all the way to the cross. He didn't stop when He heard He would have to endure the hell of being separated from His Father, and I believe He will give you the strength to continue on as well. Keep running, keep teaching, keep loving, keep influencing. Just....keep.....going. You may be thinking, "I can't do it!." But that's ok, if He lives in you, because His Spirit will sustain you. And rest assured He CAN do it. He has given us "a Spirit of LOVE, POWER and SELF-CONTROL"(2 Timothy 1:7). So get up and get resolved. It will be worth it. He promises.

WEEK 2

Get Over The Hump Day LESSONS LEARNED FROM COLLEGE FOOTBALL Devotional:

You CAN choose to be stupid. When I was in high school, one of my favorite things to do was to play backyard football. You would never be able to tell by looking at me, but my bones were strong and I was fast. I was also about 100 pounds, so I had to prove myself over and over and over again. However, I was just stupid enough to not be afraid of anything or anyone. And I had the smart mouth to prove it. God watched over me, as I deserved a beating many times but narrowly escaped (thank you to all my large protective friends from back in the day). We played football with no pads, and guys came home with broken ribs, fingers, etc. Thankfully I escaped broken bones. I did lose a big toenail running in a touchdown barefoot. Yep, that's a fact. But I've already said I was stupid, so no more explanation needed. I did a lot of stupid things back then, and I still do some to this day. But it's a lot less than it used to be because of the wisdom I'm gaining through my walk with God. That said, I don't think if I knew I was going to get to play in The College Football National Championship Game that I would do anything that might put that opportunity in jeopardy. So it will always surprise me, even when it shouldn't, that someone would throw away a great opportunity for one moment of a meaningless high. That happens way too many times, but I'm specifically remembering how in 2015 some of the players missed out on the National Championship game because they used drugs. And this verse came to my mind as my friend preached on it just the other day.

PROVERBS 30:1-9

The man declares, I am weary, O God;
I am weary, O God, and worn out.
2
Surely I AM TOO STUPID TO BE A MAN.
I have not the understanding of a man.
3
I have not learned wisdom,
nor have I knowledge of the Holy One.
4
Who has ascended to heaven and come down?

Who has gathered the wind in his fists?
Who has wrapped up the waters in a garment?
Who has established all the ends of the earth?
What is his name, and what is his son's name?
Surely you know!
5
Every word of God proves true;
he is a shield to those who take refuge in him.
6
Do not add to his words,
lest he rebuke you and you be found a liar.
7
<u>Two things I ask of you</u>;
deny them not to me before I die:
8
REMOVE FAR FROM ME FALSEHOOD and lying;
give me neither poverty nor riches;
feed me with the food that is needful for me,
9

lest I be full and deny you
and say, "Who is the Lord?"
or lest I be poor and steal
and profane the name of my God.

Here's the truth. If you're a follower of Jesus, you are a minister. Ministers of the gospel are missing our National Championship every day when we choose a moment's high and become disqualified from the most important mission in the history of man and lose the respect of those within our sphere of influence. This is no game. This is real life. Stay true to your spouse. "Train" up your children. Work hard. Do not bow down to money. Let service be your natural high as you watch God work. We've all been tempted, and God has never failed us. But fantasies fail us every day. He will always take care of what we NEED. He will never leave us. He deserves to be trusted. He deserves our obedience. Think twice before you grab on to a cheap high that means nothing. It could cost you everything. Do not be

deceived, pastor, youth minister, doctor, teacher, or stay-at-home parent. Without God's wisdom guiding us, we are easily deceived. Stay on your guard, because without the wisdom of God we are stupid creatures. The proof is there. Waaaaay too much proof. Read verses 8-9 again and pray over them. God can help our stupidity if we stay close to Him. Now put on those pads, and get back out there you idiots!
(Kidding....kind of.)

WEEK 3

Get Over The Hump Day EQUALITY AND SLAVERY Devotional:

We just got out of school for MLK Day. I believe it was just a couple of years ago that one of my children looked at the calendar, which read:

"MLK Day," and asked me, "Hey daddy, why do we get out of school for milk day?" Of course I laughed and said something about chocolate milk, which went over the kids' heads. And then I explained to them who MLK was, and how we needed more leaders like him today. I reflected on my first reaction to the question, which was to make a quick joke as I thought about an obvious trait of MLK. He's an African-American. I'm not sure what I am....Irish, Scottish, Cherokee Indian (Native American for the PC crowd) is what I've been told. But to anyone who sees me, I'm white. And that's more obvious when I jump (another stereotype joke...about whites or caucasians). Did you ever sing that song in church., "Red and yellow, black and white, they are precious in His sight, Jesus loves the little children of the world?" That's simple and correct, but now some find it offensive. And I find the fact that people find that offensive, well...offensive. Was that confusing? Well, so is this whole politically correct movement. OK, here's the truth.

GALATIANS 3:28 - There is neither Jew nor Greek, there is neither bond nor free, there is neither male nor female: for ye are all one in Christ Jesus.

COLOSSIANS 3:23-25 "And whatever you do, do it heartily, as to the Lord and not to men, knowing that from the Lord you will receive the reward of the inheritance; for you serve the Lord Christ. But he who does wrong will be repaid for what he has done, and THERE IS NO PARTIALITY ".

ROMANS 2:11 "For there is no partiality with God"

God created us all in His image, and different but equal. So we should all expect to be, well, uhm....different, but ya know.....EQUAL. I know we've made it seem complicated, but it's really not. That's what is so great about many answers in the Bible. One thing we can bank on is that God loves us, no matter what our race. He said in LUKE 10:27, "'Love the Lord your God with all your heart and with all your soul and with all your strength and with all your mind," and, "LOVE YOUR NEIGHBOR AS YOURSELF."

That about settles it, doesn't it? I've got lots of opinions on this subject, but the only thing that really matters it what the Scriptures teach. We're all loved by God (JOHN 3:16). We're all equal. We're all slaves to sin and in need of rescue (ROMANS 3:23). We all start out in the same slavery, in need of a redeemer. There has always been the horrible misuse of other people...from the Jewish people, to the African-Americans, to women all over the world being sold into the sexual slave trade. All this slavery stems from the original form of slavery. The slavery to sin. To fix the problem we must change the hearts of men by telling them The Good News of The God who can save them. The One who bought our freedom. Once we've broken free from the slavery of sin, I believe we will see all the other slavery begin to disappear under the reign of love for God and our fellow man. So maybe I'm just too simple. But if we want equality and to stop all these forms of slavery, I believe we must understand we are all under the SAME CURSE and in need of the SAME SAVIOR who offers us all the SAME SALVATION.

WEEK 4

Get Over The Hump Day WHAT IS YOUR TREASURE Devotional:

One of the greatest inventions of our time is the DVR. Yes, the DVR has kept many men from having to compromise their beliefs. Nobody wanted to tape the Super Bowl on VHS and watch it after church, so they skipped church. But with a DVR it's just like the game has been postponed until YOU can get there! This was a conviction for me in college. Of course in my younger days it was never an issue. We were at church... PERIOD. We'd always catch the second half after church. Then in college I chose to make the decision to go to church instead of see the whole game. I don't think you have to do that to be a "Real Christian," but I felt convicted to do that just to make sure I had my own personal priorities straight. I'm bringing this up now before Super Bowl Sunday so many of you will feel guilty for skipping church!!! LOL.

Ok, here's the real reason I bring this up. Priorities show up in the little decisions we make every day. The decisions we make show very clearly what our priorities are, although we may not see it ourselves because "The heart is deceitful above all things, and desperately wicked: who can know it?" (JEREMIAH 17:9) And we tend to be blind to our own priority problems.

Sooner or later your priorities will become evident, "For where your treasure is, there will your heart be also." (LUKE 12:34). If God is your treasure, it will show. If you love your wife and kids the right way, it will show both when you are there and when you can't be there. If money, fame, power, or work are your priority, then that will also show. I think we understand as Christians what our priorities "should" be. "And he said to him, "You shall love the Lord your God with all your heart and with all your soul and with all your mind. This is the great and first commandment." (MATTHEW 22:37-38)

The question I'm daring us to ask ourselves is: WHAT ARE OUR PRIORITIES? Or a better question might be: What would others say our priorities are, based on what our actions show? If I were to ask your husband, wife, kids, or pastor what your priorities are, what would they say? Remember this in EXODUS 20:3 "You shall have no other gods before me." Would you rather be with your brothers and sisters in Christ worshipping the One True, Righteous, Awesome, All Powerful God, or would you rather be sitting on the couch watching some dudes throw around a deflated ball?(Tom Brady joke). Or out fishing on the lake He created? I'm using these stereotypical events as an example to point out one thing: We can all say "I've got my priorities in line. I believe in God, Family, and Work." But actions speak louder than words. If you golf with your buddies 3 weekends out of 4 and haven't taken your kids to a movie, or hiking, or to get pizza, you're putting golfing with the boys before your family. And it's obvious. Go ask someone who will be honest with you what they think your priorities are, and try not to be defensive. LISTEN CLOSELY. Then go and get down on your knees and bow to The One who is most worthy of our time and attention. Give thanks for His help, ask forgiveness, or do whatever He leads you to do. Let's get our priorities in line. Let's get our conscience clear. Then let's go make an impact on the lives of others. Enjoy that Super Bowl, but make sure you enjoy your God more. He will never cheat you or leave you deflated. (repeated Tom Brady joke).

WEEK 5

Get Over The Hump Day WRONG DECISION Devotional:

If you watched or heard about Super Bowl 49, you'll know where I got the title for this devotion. If you didn't, here's a short synopsis of what happened: The Seattle Seahawks played the New England Patriots. The game was tied at halftime 14-14. Seattle built a 10 point lead to end the third quarter. The Patriots rallied to take the lead in the 4th quarter 28-24 with about 2 minutes left in the game. Seattle then drives down the field all the way to the Patriots 1 yard line. Seattle has the best running back in the league. They call him "BEAST MODE" because he's a BEAST!. There are 26 seconds left on the clock, and they have the ball on the 1 yard line with the best running back in the league. And what does Seattle do? They run the ball in for the touchdown and the win.....NOT! They call a pass play that gets intercepted!!! Yeah, you read that right. I'll never understand that call.....ever.....never, ever. Although that was the worst play call I've ever seen in my lifetime, I'm not the one who has had to live with it. And it was not a sin! Coach Carroll can rest easy knowing he can account to God for his decision. I know Seattle fans probably think it was a sin, but I assure you it was not. However, making the decision to disobey God is and will always be a sin and is much worse than losing a big-time over-hyped game. Life is not a game. It's so much more. Every decision counts and has an impact on someone.

I have waaay too many personal stories to share on this subject. Fights in my marriage, missed moments with my kids, and missed blessings that I could have had by doing something for others. All the selfish decisions I've made begin to mount up as I think about how many times my Loving yet Mighty Powerful Warrior God and Father has forgiven me for making the wrong decisions. I'm sure you understand where I'm coming from, so let's consider two things today.

FIRST: Understanding our failures and how to overcome them. We have all failed. We have all sinned and fallen short (ROMANS 3:23). We fight a spiritual battle everyday if we are believers. We, as a family of believers, fight against the sins of selfishness, laziness, pride, lust, envy, greed, etc. every day. (ROMANS 6:12-13 - Let not sin therefore reign in your mortal body, to make you obey its passions. Do not present your members to sin as instruments for unrighteousness, but present yourselves to God as those who have been brought from death to life, and your members to God as instruments for righteousness.) We can't go into battle without a strategy. We go to our Warrior of a God (EXODUS 15:3 - The LORD is a warrior; The LORD is His name) and ask for His help for each day. We get our mind set straight and we ask for wisdom from the One who gives it to us without hesitation (JAMES 1:5 -But if any of you lacks wisdom, let him ask of God, who gives to all generously and without reproach, and it will be given to him.) And if we fall during battle, we cry out to our Merciful Leader (DEUTERONOMY 4:31a -For the LORD your God is a merciful God...) who will forgive us He will save us and pick us up, and defend us and set us back upon our feet so we can fight again. This is the life we've chosen. To live to please The One who deserves to be worshipped and praised (PSALM

96:1-13), and most importantly, Obeyed. (JOHN 14:23 -Jesus replied, "Anyone who loves me will obey my teaching. My Father will love them, and we will come to them and make our home with them.) He is The Head of our family, The Great God and Father and Author and Finisher of our Faith. Go to Him each day. That is how we both gain understanding and forgiveness for our sins and wrong decisions.

SECOND: We tell others where they are failing and how to overcome it. This will require a lot of prayer and a lot of practice and a ton of love and concern for others. No one likes to be told that they are in sin, or that they are consistently making the wrong decisions. However, as a family of believers we are to encourage and help each other overcome sin. (HEBREWS 10:24 -And let us consider how to stir up one another to love and good works. JAMES 5:16 - Therefore, confess your sins to one another and pray for one another, that you may be healed. The prayer of a righteous person has great power as it is working. PROVERBS 27:17 - Iron sharpens iron, and one man sharpens another.) I once heard a friend say that "We should not go to others with God until we've gone to God about others." The point here is PRAYER. Pray for them before we confront them. MATTHEW 18 is pretty clear about how to approach a believer who is in sin. Follow that model with a heart full of love and understanding. Remember to treat them as you would want to be treated (LUKE 6:31 - Do unto others....) and pray for their restoration.

As believers we will all make some bad decisions. We all sin, but we're all part of the same family and take care of each other. We look out for our weaker brothers and sisters and strengthen them in the faith. We pray together and sing praises to Our Strong Worthy Creator. We're all in this together. Forgive and be forgiven, and stand together in THE FAITH. Maybe you've made a terrible decision. It's ok. Your family will help you through the consequences of that decision and guide you back to Our Father who is ready and waiting to Forgive You. Because that's the kind of Dad that HE IS.

Oh and if you're ever in the Super Bowl and you have one of the best running backs in the league and you have the ball at the 1 yard line….run the ball.

WEEK 6

Get Over The Hump Day VALENTINE Devotional:

What is Love? (baby don't hurt me, don't hurt me no more....)

I've stated openly before that I did not do dating correctly. There are better ways to find a mate than treating each other like new clothing... trying each other out like we're buying clothes, and then when it's getting old we throw it out and look for something new. This subject deserves its own devotional, so I'll stop short of the subject of dating for now and launch right into the subject of LOVE. This is a simple idea that goes deeper than we could ever imagine. But here it is: LOVE IS NOT A FEELING. I'll say it again: LOVE IS NOT A FEELING. This was part of my struggle in dating. When you're friends with someone of the opposite sex, and you really like that person, you gain affectionate feelings for that person. You might even love that person, but it may not be in a marital way. But you have these....."feelings". Example: If you have a sister, you have feelings for that sister. You also love her very much, but that doesn't mean you would make out with her (even if you're from Alabama. Sorry, had to get that in there. Maybe I should say Roll Tide to make it better....). So remember that we are Brothers and Sisters in Christ. Feelings often lead us in the wrong direction and confuse us.

God never leads us down the wrong road or attempts to confuse His children. We get confused because our society (led by our enemy) has twisted the idea of what love and affection really is, and how it should be used. Let's define LOVE from The Holy Word of God.

(1 JOHN 4:7-8 Beloved, let us love one another: for love is of God; and every one that loveth is born of God, and knoweth God. He that loveth not knoweth not God; for GOD IS LOVE.)

Did you read that last line? Love has been defined as God Himself. GOD IS LOVE. Therefore it's clear that anything HE is not in can NOT be love. IF IT IS AGAINST HIS WORD, IT CANNOT BE LOVE. That will answer a lot of your questions concerning certain situations in life such as sex outside marriage, homosexuality, reading certain books, or watching movies based on the aforementioned subjects. (1 CORINTHIANS 6:9-11 Or do you not know that wrongdoers will not inherit the kingdom of God? DO NOT BE DECEIVED: Neither the sexually immoral nor idolaters nor adulterers nor men who have sex with men, nor thieves nor the greedy nor drunkards nor slanderers nor swindlers will inherit the kingdom of God. And that is what some of you WERE. But you were WASHED, you were SANCTIFIED, you were JUSTIFIED in the name of THE LORD JESUS CHRIST and by THE SPIRIT OF our GOD.)

There can be no actual love in those things, because God is not in those things. If you disagree with me here, it makes no difference. If you hate what I'm saying, it simply doesn't matter. Feel free to ignore my opinion. It's not worth much, but this is God's Word, and it's The Way To Life and True Love. Please don't ignore it. The Word of God is True and Clear. The Bible doesn't say whatever we "want" it to be saying. It says what it says. God is indeed love. There is no love in the back seat of that car no matter how much "love" is professed. God isn't in it. Therefore, there is no love in it. March all day and night long about how you feel, but feelings do not change The Truth. I don't feel it's right to be taxed so highly, but if I don't pay my taxes the truth is that I will go to jail.

We have downgraded love into something cheaper. Flippant words to put into songs, or just a phrase to express our feelings based on getting something we want. Love seeks to give others what they need. Jesus never needed a sexual relationship. He was tempted. (HEBREWS 4:15 For we do not have a high priest who is unable to sympathize with our weaknesses, but one who in every respect has been tempted as we are, yet without sin). But it wasn't something to be attained for Him. Not because it was bad (within marriage it's quite enjoyable), but because it wasn't necessary for love. The strongest and truest LOVE has absolutely nothing to do with getting physical. It's about being sacrificial. The reason we love is to honor God, not to please our bodies (1 CORINTHIANS 6:12-17 "I have the right to do anything," you say—but not everything is beneficial. "I have the right to do anything"—but I will not be mastered by anything. You say, "Food for the stomach and the stomach for food, and God will destroy them both." THE BODY, however, IS NOT MEANT FOR SEXUAL IMMORALITY BUT FOR THE LORD, and the Lord for the body. By his power God raised the Lord from the dead, and he will raise us also. Do you not know that your bodies are members of Christ himself? Shall I then take the members of Christ and unite them with a prostitute? Never! Do you not know that he who unites himself with a prostitute is one with her in body? For it is said, "The two will become one flesh." But whoever is united with the Lord is one with him in spirit.).

OK believers. I'm not making feelings the enemy here, but someone somewhere long ago decided to twist the meaning of love into something cheaper, and it's time we take back the meaning of Real Love. Do you Love God? There is a way to show it. (JOHN 14:21 Whoever has my commandments and keeps them, he it is who loves me. And he who loves me will be loved by my Father, and I will love him and manifest myself to him.") According to God's Word, if you LOVE HIM, you will OBEY HIM. Read The Word and be discerning. Put down that book ladies. Turn off that computer men. Love can't be found in the fantasy world by stirring up your feelings. It will be found by doing for others what Christ has done for us. Sacrificing our time and energy to do things that obey God and make a difference in others' lives. Jesus showed us what LOVE IS. JOHN 3:16 For God so LOVED the world that He GAVE. Yeah, it's harder work, but sooooo much more fulfilling. I write this out of a spirit of love for my brothers and sisters in Christ. Have a great Valentine's Day, and know this....God Loves You!!

In the writing of this I realized that I used to think I loved Chick-Fil-A. But the truth is that I would never sacrifice my life for the store (Sorry Chick-Fil-A), and must admit I just had feelings for its food. Those feelings are real and definitely ok, but I wouldn’t call it true love. Although it feels like it sometimes.......

WEEK 7

Get Over The Hump Day ASKING QUESTIONS Devotional:

Have you ever heard of a man proposing to a woman by getting down on one knee and asking, "Where will you marry me?" Or "I'm not sure why I want to marry you, but will you marry me?" Those seem to be strange questions. Now I don't want to take up the entire day covering all the strange questions in the world, or even all the good ones. Frankly we couldn't cover them all in a day, or even a week or more. However, I do want to shed light on the subject of ASKING QUESTIONS.

Social media exists because of the question "What If?" You know, like, "Hey Billy, what if you jump off the roof onto that trampoline and I film it? You think people would watch it?" "I don't know, Randy, let's try it. Then you set yourself on fire, and we'll try to put it out with a bottle of lotion." You know, that kind of stuff. My children ask me questions all the time: "Can we get a dog?" "Can we watch a movie?" "Are there witches in heaven?" Yeah, that last one is a real question from one of my kids. I had just described heaven as best I could. I felt I'd done a pretty good job. I was kind of patting myself on the back, and then that's the question I got. It kind of deflated me at that moment, but we prayed together and I went back to my bedroom to tell my wife the story. As I recall, we got some really good laughs from it. (In case anyone is out there wondering...Witches won't be in heaven flying around on brooms.) Kids... gotta love em. I do let my kids know that they can ask me questions. I encourage it. I've heard people say that there are no stupid questions, but I can't bring myself to agree with that because I've heard some really dumb ones in my day. Parents, you know what I mean. But I even let my kids know that those are also allowed. Where do you think I get most of my material??

Some of our questions may be silly. They may be selfish, or maybe they're really good ones. God allows us to ask them all. That amazes me. I know God. He cares for me and you, and He hears His children. The God of the universe hears me. He hears you. If you are His child, He hears you. WOW! He puts up with silly questions. He allows us to express our feelings, and He wants to speak to us through His Word. So ASK QUESTIONS as you read The

Word, and then be prepared for the answer. There are different answers that we find in scripture. I will point out three.

#1: I think of John the Baptist sending his friends to ask Jesus if He really is The One. John received the answer he was hoping for. YES! HE IS! Deaf people are hearing, blind people are seeing, the lame can walk, and the dead are being raised. So sometimes we get the answer for which we were hoping. (MATTHEW 11:1-6)

#2 I think of the disciples fighting over who would be the greatest. Jesus stepped into the conversation, and answered the question: "What does it take to be great?" The answer was not what they wanted or expected to hear. I imagine if we're fighting over which of us is the greatest, then we're probably not thinking about how we can best serve each other. However, according to Jesus, if you want to be great, then you will serve others. He gave the example by washing their feet. Doing the "lowly" jobs. "Doing unto others". So sometimes we get an answer, but it's not the kind of answer we expect. (LUKE 22:24-26)

#3 I think of Job. Ok, I'm gonna give Job a pass. If anyone deserved to ask the question, "Why Me?" or "What's going on?" it would be Job. His story has always intrigued me. I wrote a one act play on the life of Job. It's called Behemoth, and it's a comedy. I know, I'm strange. Job did have questions. "Why is this happening?" "Why was I born?" (JOB 3) I'm going to stop myself from spending the next half hour talking about Job and just say this... He never got an answer to his question! That's right. God instead asks him questions. Two to three chapters worth of questions that Job couldn't answer. And Job responded correctly by saying, "I'm sorry. You are God and I am not." (That's a paraphrase). So sometimes we don't get an answer to our questions no matter how legitimate the questions may be. We are reminded in the book of Job of God's sovereignty, and that although He is a merciful and loving heavenly Father, He doesn't owe us answers to our questions. We're not entitled to answers, but we take refuge in the fact that HE IS COMPLETELY IN CHARGE AND HE LOVES US AND WANTS WHAT IS BEST FOR US. (JOB 38-42)

I've lost family members and friends way too early. I've lost great opportunities that I just knew God was lining up for me, but they didn't work out. I've given up on dreams and created new ones, and failed to reach goals that I'd hoped to reach. I've had a lot of questions for God. Some of them were stupid, but I know He heard me. As I read His word, I feel like the one answer I get from Him every day is this: Yes, Jackson (insert your own name here), I do love you. I do care about you, and about the questions you have. I may not answer them, but you may ask them. I will hear you, and I will care. They may be dumb questions, but you may ask them. They may be selfish ones, but I will guide you to a point where you ask those questions less and less, and learn to ask questions according to MY WILL and for MY GLORY. (1 JOHN 5:14-15).

So ask questions. Maybe you'll get the answer for which you hoped. Maybe you'll get an answer that you didn't expect. Maybe you won't get an answer at all. Just remember that HE IS IN CONTROL and HE CARES. Take some time today to ask a question. Search the scriptures for answers, and know that HE IS LISTENING.

PSALMS 65:2 (NASB)
O You who hear prayer,
To You all men come.
PSALMS 34:15 (NASB)
The eyes of the Lord are toward the righteous
And His ears are open to their cry.
PROVERBS 15:29 (NASB)
The Lord is far from the wicked,
But He hears the prayer of the righteous.
2 CHRONICLES 7:14-15 (ESV)
if my people who are called by my name humble themselves, and pray and seek my face and turn from their wicked

ways, then I will hear from heaven and
will forgive their sin and heal their land.
15 Now my eyes will be open and my
ears attentive to the prayer that is made
in this place.
PSALMS 66:19-20 (NASB)
But certainly God has heard;
He has given heed to the voice of my
prayer.
20 Blessed be God,
Who has not turned away my prayer
Nor His lovingkindness from me.

WEEK 8

Get Over The Hump Day OMG Devotional:

Thou shalt not take the name of the Lord thy God in vain; for the Lord will not hold him guiltless that taketh his name in vain.

EXODUS 20:7

I was a teenager, and I was riding with my dad over to my granddad's house. When we pulled into the driveway, I made a comment about praying. I don't remember what we were talking about. I only remember that I wanted to say something about praying to God. For some reason I felt a little strange about making the statement (probably because I was an awkward teenage boy, and if you know one of these creatures they tend to feel and be awkward). I said something to the effect of "taking my concerns to the big man upstairs." I'm sure I was trying to say something in a "cool" way. My dad seemed offended. He paused for a few moments, and then began to help me understand that there are better ways to address and refer to our God. The conversation didn't last long, but it's never left me. And I never referred to God again as "the man upstairs," because at that moment my eyes were opened to how inadequate and inappropriate that was when talking about my Holy, Righteous, Divine, Heavenly Father. I hope to make a similar impact right now to anyone out there who professes to be a follower of Jesus. There are many ways that are inappropriate when talking about God, but one in particular that has made its way into even the Christian's common vocabulary is the phrase "Oh My God." And that has now been shortened and made popular as "OMG." I'm asking all of you reading this to help me get the word out. God's name deserves to be honored, not used as if it were something you toss away after using it. Here are some things to consider and to share:

HOW DO THE SCRIPTURES REFER TO GOD?

GOD THE FATHER:

God Most High (GENESIS 14:18)
Our Shield (PSALM 59:11)
Holy One (PSALM 71:22)
God of Heaven (NEHEMIAH 1:5)
Great and Awesome God (NEHEMIAH 1:5)
My Strength (PSALM 59:9)
My Loving God (PSALM 59:10)
God Who Avenges (PSALM 94:1)
Judge of the Earth (PSALM 94:2)
Abba, Father (MARK 14:36)
Only True God (JOHN 17:3)

God of Peace (I THESSALONIANS 5:23)
God the Blessed and Only Sovereign (1 TIMOTHY 6:15)
God of all Grace (1 PETER 5:10)
GOD THE SON
Master (LUKE 17:13)
Son of Man (LUKE 19:10)
The Resurrection and the Life (JOHN 11:25)
Teacher and Lord (JOHN 13:13)
Way, the Truth, and the Life (JOHN 14:6)
Bread of Life (JOHN 6:35)
True Vine (JOHN 15:1)
Our high priest (HEBREWS 5:10)
GOD THE SPIRIT
Spirit of Truth (JOHN 16:13)
Spirit of Holiness (ROMANS 1:4)
Spirit of Life (ROMANS 8:2)
Eternal Spirit (HEBREWS 9:14)

HOW DO THE DEMONS ADDRESS THE SAVIOR?
MARK 1:24 (NIV)
24 "What do you want with us, Jesus of Nazareth? Have you come to destroy

us? I know who you are—THE HOLY ONE OF GOD!"

MARK 3:11 (ASV)

And the unclean spirits, whensoever they beheld him, fell down before him, and cried, saying, THOU ARE THE SON OF GOD.

HOW SHOULD WE ADDRESS GOD? Here's some insight...

EXODUS 20:7

"You shall not take the name of the LORD your God in vain, for the LORD will not leave him unpunished who takes His name in vain.

(The word "vain" means "for no reason" or "useless." God was instructing the Israelites to avoid using His name in a useless, disrespectful way.)

MATTHEW 12:36-37, Jesus says: "But I say to you that for every idle word men may speak, they will give account of it in the day of judgment. For by your words you will be justified and by your words you will be condemned."

The words we use are important. How we speak about God is of the utmost importance. So, Christians, OMG HAS NO PLACE IN YOUR VOCABULARY. It bothers me how many churchgoers seem to throw out the phrase “Oh My God” in a way that does not honor or worship Him at all. Vain words. Idle words. If you’re a believer, then I’m your brother. And as your brother I’m asking my spiritual family members to see me as that weaker brother to whom you are offending when you use that phrase. Start listening. You’ll hear others use it without one thought of The Savior who died for them. Use that list above. Address Him as The God of Heaven, or Master, or The God of all Grace, or The Spirit of Truth and Holiness. Even as Abba Father, or Friend. HE IS a Mighty Warrior, HE IS a Loving Father, HE IS KING, HE IS LORD and HE IS WORTHY TO BE PRAISED! Let the old song be a reminder... “Oh be careful little tongue what you say.” And if your lips ever utter that OMG phrase, I pray it’s because you’re addressing THE HOLY ONE and not because you’re excited about the new movie that just came out. The next time you speak, remember that The God of the universe is listening. Address Him accordingly.

WEEK 9

Get Over The Hump Day RUNNING OUT OF TIME Devotional:

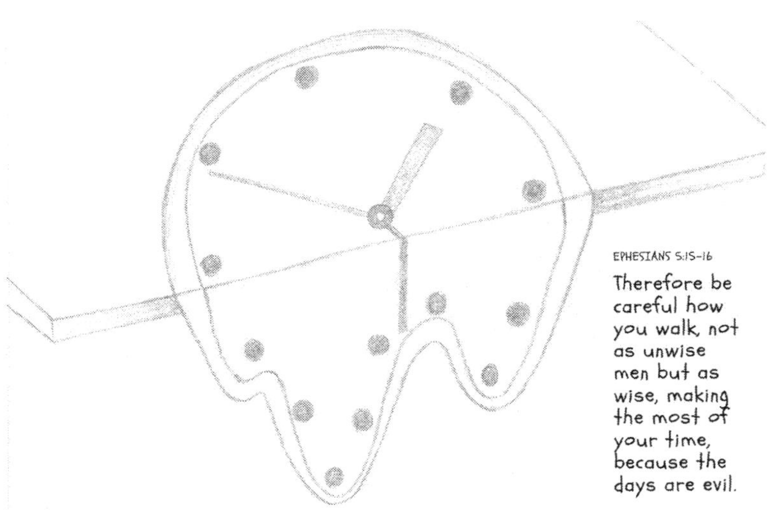

The other day I knew the entire family needed to take a shower within the next hour or so, and we all know what that means. Get there FIRST! Whoever is last will run out of hot water, and knowing that is a powerful motivator. Sometimes the only thing that could make me jump out of bed was when I knew there was going to be a line for the shower. There's nothing as bad as that feeling of your hot water fading away. You get into a nice hot shower, and the water gets a little cooler. So you naturally turn up the heat. Now you've put shampoo in your hair, and it gets cooler. And you think, "Please no, no please...NO, don't do this to me!" What started out as the most wonderful feeling is fading away. And as much as you want to enjoy this moment and relax, you know you must rinse and repeat as fast as possible before time runs out! Talk about water torture!!! That's pretty much the feeling we get while raising our children isn't it? They're growing. Another year just flew by. Looking at photos from just last year, my kids look so small... so much like....well, kids. Now they look like young adults, and the water keeps getting colder and colder. And we feel like we must make the most of every moment before time runs out on us.

We need to work. We need computers these days. We have responsibilities. All this is true, but more importantly we also have friendships, spouses, children, and time we need to spend with our Savior. What are our priorities? Well, the truth is that all these things have their place. The question is, what place do we give them? This is a devotion, and I wish I had more time to explore this subject with you. But since time is brief, I'll just quote this: (EPHESIANS 5:15-16 Therefore be careful how you walk, not as unwise men but as wise, MAKING THE MOST OF YOUR TIME, because the days are evil.)

I can't make blanket statements on jobs. Some people work crazy schedules, and a man must provide for his family (1 TIMOTHY 5:8). I have a weird schedule, but I fight to plan things and make time to hang out with my family. This is just a simple reminder that no one on their deathbed ever says, "I wish I could spend a few more hours at work," or "If only I could buy one more thing." What we all think about when it comes down to crunch time is that we wish we'd spent more time with the ones we love. There are people you haven't spoken to in years out there. Pick up the phone and make that call today. You've promised your son or daughter you'd practice ball with them or take them out to dinner. Stop putting it off and go get that baseball glove. I don't care if it's raining. If it is you'll create a memory for your child they will never forget. Take pictures, be silly, #LAUGHMORE with your family. This life is like being in a shower that's running out of hot water. It's gone before we know it. I think that making the most of our time is done by making an impact on those around us. So here's a simple reminder to do things that you know will GLORIFY GOD and HELP OTHERS in some way. Don't put off your family. Make that call, go on that date, make that apology. Stop making decisions based on your feelings, and start making them based on what you know needs to be done. Make The Most Of Your Time!!! Now! Go!!!

WEEK 10

Get Over The Hump Day EPIC FAIL Devotional:

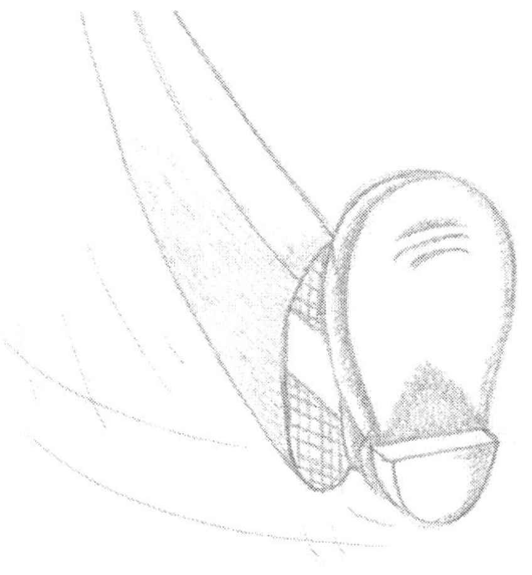

EPIC FAIL

for ALL have sinned....

ROMANS 3:23

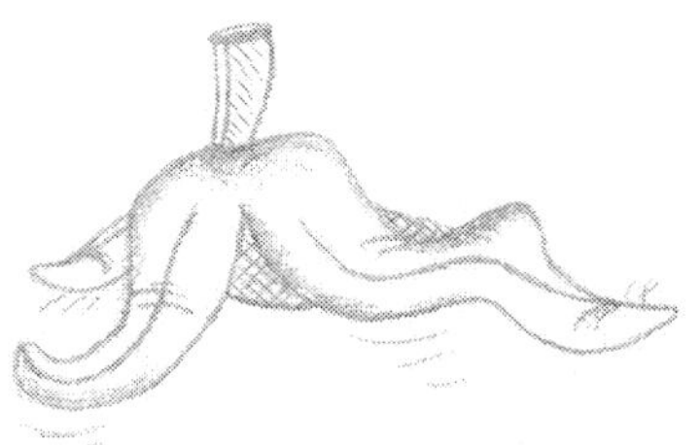

I am a failure. There's not a lot of people who actually feel like a success, is there? If there were, then they wouldn't be working so hard to "make it" in the business (whatever business it might be and whatever "making it"

actually means.) Millions of people each day are trying to grasp their 15 minutes of fame on TV or Youtube, and they'll do just about anything to get it. I'll never forget the time I entered a dance contest. I was jumping up and down like I knew what I was doing, trying to get picked. Uhm...they pointed at me, and the next thing I knew I was on stage......totally unprepared. I was young and foolish, and I couldn't really dance. Now I've learned a few things since then, but at the time, well....let's just say I had five left feet! When it came my turn, I tried to be funny. But what I know now was that these people were serious about their dancing, and needless to say, I got booed off the stage!! I'd like to say there were only about 10 people in the crowd, but there were about 1,000. Of course it's hilarious now, but at the time I felt like a failure. Because obviously, I had failed.

I was thinking today about what a failure I've been in so many areas. Business, marriage, parenting...I fail every day. Even the fact that I've been meaning to hang a shelf for about 3 weeks reminds me of my failure to do so every time I pass that area of my house. I thought about Robin Williams last night. He should be a success story, right? I mean, a comedian with accolades for both comedy and drama whom almost everyone seemed to love. He had plenty of work lined up, millions of followers on social media sites, and plenty of money. What's not successful about that? And still he fought depression. And so will we at some point in our lives. Maybe some not as severe as others, but at some point in your life you will probably feel like a failure. And I'm here to tell you that it's ok, because what you think is success might not be success after all. Sometimes we need the darkness to show how bright the light is, or a bad meal to help us remember how the good ones taste. Speaking of taste... Read this:

(PSALM 34:8 ESV - Oh, taste and see that the Lord is good! Blessed is the man who takes refuge in him)

We must take refuge in Him. Here's the good news: We're ALL failures!!! Case in point:

(ROMANS 3:23 ESV - for all have sinned and fall short of the glory of God...)

If you ever wonder why you feel like a failure sometimes, it's because you are. And so am I. And that's not a bad thing unless you stay there wallowing in your failure. You are a success story waiting to happen!! No, you won't find real life success in that 15 min of fame, or an award, or a great job, or a raise. And you may fight these feelings and misconceptions for a long time. Let's take a break from all that worry, and feel the wind in our face for a few minutes together here as we recall some important information that hopefully will always come rushing to our minds in our moments of feeling as if we've failed. First of all, we need to know that when we've failed spiritually there is HOPE:

(1 JOHN 1:9 ESV - If we confess our sins, HE IS FAITHFUL and just to

FORGIVE US our sins and to CLEANSE US from all unrighteousness.)
and remember

(PROVERBS 28:13 ESV - Whoever conceals his transgressions will not prosper, but HE WHO CONFESSES AND FORSAKES THEM WILL OBTAIN MERCY.)

There is success available. Success in life starts by knowing Christ Jesus. You will find Forgiveness and Mercy in Christ if you run to Him for refuge. He will cleanse you. You can start over and over and over again. In knowing Him, your life will find purpose. And that is where finding success begins. When we fail, the enemy would have us to live in secret and in shame, and to be defeated by our feelings and hide (remember Adam and Eve). Hiding isn't the answer, unless you're hiding in the cleft of THE ROCK. Run to Him. Take Refuge. Receive what He promises and be cleansed. Breathe in His Love. Be forgiven. Enjoy His mercy. Success in life begins with finding a purpose. Whether you've failed spiritually or just simply lost a dancing contest. Get up and realize that the important thing is that you put this verse into action:

(1 CORINTHIANS 10:31 - whether you eat or drink, or whatever you do, do all to the glory of God.) That is where success is found.

By the way, I just hung that shelf.

WEEK 11

Get Over The Hump Day
DISAPPOINTMENT Devotional:

I was living in Orlando, FL, and I was working at Universal Studios. I worked on the Jaws ride. I worked hard. I even left my blood out there, literally! The blood story is for a different day, but while working I heard there were auditions for a part in one of the shows. The Terminator 2 show was up and running and they were having tryouts for the part of the T2. I went out for the part. It was a Saturday afternoon, and I arrived and stood in line for what seemed like days. A few hours later they finally called my name. There were about 30 of us standing in a line facing the man who was making the decision. He looked at me and walked over to me and asked for my resume, which I gladly handed him. I was feeling pretty good as he scribbled something on it and handed it back to me. I couldn't read it, but I was sure I had been noticed. I kind of looked around thinking, "yeah, he asked to see MY resume, not yours or yours or yours" as I was pointing at the competition in my mind. After they looked us over for about 10-15 minutes, they started at one end of the line, and like duck duck goose started tapping people on the head to leave (Ok, they didn't really tap us on the head. They just pointed at us). He made it over to me and stopped. I'm not kidding. He stopped. He didn't stop at anyone else. He didn't ask to see any one else's resume. I knew the job was mine. He finally looked at me and said, "Nice try man, but you're too short." It was over. The entire day was spent just to hear someone tell me I was too short for the part.

That's just one story, people. I have many more that sound a lot like that, and you probably do too. So......

Have you ever been disappointed with God? Maybe that's where you are right now. It may be hard to admit it, but I'm pretty sure it happens to all of us at some point. The truth is I'm pretty embarrassed as I write this thinking about how many times I've thought things should all turn out my way, and I went into God's throne room and there in the midst of His Magnificent Presence I stood with my bottom lip sticking out. Yes, that thing we discipline our kids for seems ok when it's us, doesn't it? Yeah, my kid didn't make the team, but I told him to stop his whining. One week later you don't get that promotion, and we learn where our kids learn it from. It's natural. However, as believers we want to be doing and acting in a way that is

SUPERnatural. The only way to do that is to be walking in The Spirit each and every day. It is that Spirit in us that allows us to rejoice in any circumstance.
ROMANS 5:3-5
"We can rejoice, too, when we run into problems and trials, for we know that they help us develop endurance. And endurance develops strength of character, and character strengthens our confident hope of salvation. AND THIS HOPE WILL NOT LEAD TO DISAPPOINTMENT. For we know how dearly GOD LOVES US, because HE HAS GIVEN US THE HOLY SPIRIT to fill our hearts with his love." (NLT)

God cares. God hears His children. He is a Merciful Gracious Father. He has every right to destroy us for our pride as we whine about what He has ordained. Instead He says in ROMANS 8:28 - And we know that God causes everything to work together for the good of those who love God and are called according to His purpose for them. Remember also that:

ISAIAH 55:8-9 - "My thoughts are not your thoughts," says The Lord. "And My ways are far beyond anything you could imagine. For just as the heavens are higher than the earth, so my ways are higher than your ways and my thoughts higher than your thoughts."

There will be times when we find ourselves disappointed with the way things have gone, but God has a plan and a purpose and He will work things out for our good. Just remember this: His desire for you in this life is more about you being Holy than it is about you being Happy. Job is a great example. God Himself pointed Job out to the enemy (JOB 1:8). Job was considered a righteous man (JOB 1:1), yet he was tested. And during that time he was clearly not happy, but held on during very hard and disappointing circumstances (JOB 1:20-22) and was restored in God's time (JOB 42:10). We will also be restored if we hold on to The One who wants what's best for us so much that He sent His Only Son here to die for us so that we could be saved

(JOHN 3:16). Take a moment and think about what Jesus Christ has done for you and watch your disappointment begin to fade.

WEEK 12

Get Over The Hump Day PATIENCE Devotional:

but they who WAIT FOR THE LORD shall renew their strength

Isaiah 40:31

I'm writing this devotion from our plane at the Chicago airport. We were delayed because of the snow. I stood in line for an hour to get my kids airline tickets because they had labeled them "unaccompanied minors." Clearly we were all there together, and they WERE "accompanied." But because someone made an error, I stood in a line for an hour. (We all had carry-on bags, or I would have had to go get in a longer line to get my bags checked through to Atlanta.) Then I got in yet another line, where a man clearly tried to cut line by stepping right in front of me. I wanted to be assertive yet kind, not forceful, and also not just passive. One thing I was having serious trouble being, though, was patient. It was very clear that I wasn't the only person having this issue. But it was also clear that as a Christian I've been given a Spirit of Love, Power, and SELF-CONTROL (2 TIMOTHY 1:7). I expect myself to behave accordingly, but many times I fail miserably. As a comedian, I was all of a sudden not finding things as funny as I usually do. All of a sudden LOL meant something totally different to me. Instead of Laugh Out Loud, it was more like Let's Obliterate Losers. At least that's the way I felt. But this was about NOT being controlled by emotions, wasn't it?

On top of all this, we had loud talkers and weird people all around us, and more than ever I just wanted to get on a plane. The guy behind us was telling people they're "cute" in a weirdo kind of way, and the lady in front of us was telling everyone in earshot (which is everyone in the airport) her feelings. Weirdo then told another two ladies they were gorgeous, and then they invited him to talk with them. Why are people so drunk and foolish, but more importantly, why do they have to be around my family right now?!?! The language was such that we moved to a different spot, and I talked with my children about avoiding the foolishness of this world. SIGH.....We are in this world but trying not to be "of it" (JOHN 17:16). However, I can't just run away, because I desire to be salt. And salt isn't preserving if it's in the cabinet. I also want to be light, so others can see my light shine. And that can't happen if my impatience bursts forth (MATTHEW 5:13-16). We are finally on the plane, and the ladies behind us are inebriated and loud. and so here we are, delayed on the runway for over an hour. I'm crying inside.

So how are you dealing with the delays of life? I once heard someone say not to ask God for patience because you might get it. While that is a cute quip, it's not very wise. Because patience is something we all need, and we should never be afraid to ask for what we "need". After all, according to 1 CORINTHIANS LOVE IS PATIENT. I wonder how many young couples have that read at their marriage ceremony just because they think it's a beautiful passage, but never actually listen to it? In a world of "hurry up" and "I want it now," patience is an even greater virtue. Here are some verses to meditate on today. Yes, MEDITATE on them. Can you find the time to do that? Here they are:

EPHESIANS 4:2 ESV

With all humility and gentleness, with patience, bearing with one another in love...

(How many of you need that verse at work or at home right now?!?! Put it into action.)

ISAIAH 40:31 ESV

But they who wait for the Lord shall renew their strength; they shall mount up with wings like eagles; they shall run and not be weary; they shall walk and not faint.

(How many times have you heard this verse? Did you know it's still true?)

ROMANS 12:12 ESV

Rejoice in hope, be patient in tribulation, be constant in prayer.

(Are you still being constant in prayer? No one promised it'd be easy.)

ROMANS 8:25 ESV

But if we hope for what we do not see, we wait for it with patience.

(Do you still look for Him to come back? Cause HE IS COMING BACK!)

GALATIANS 6:9 ESV

And let us not grow weary of doing good, for in due season we will reap, if we do not give up.

(Are you tired of doing for others? Go to the beach and get reenergized cause you're work isn't done yet!)

PSALM 37:7-9 ESV

Be still before the Lord and wait patiently for him; fret not yourself over the one who prospers in his way, over the man who carries out evil devices! Refrain from anger, and forsake wrath! Fret not yourself; it tends only to evil. For the evildoers shall be cut off, but those who wait for the Lord shall inherit the land.

(You remember that they did get the land right? And that they forgot who gave it to them....Is that us? Do we think we deserve what we've been given and are therefore impatient? We don't deserve it. Be Thankful for it and patient.)

JAMES 5:8 ESV

You also, be patient. Establish your hearts, for the coming of the Lord is at hand.

(Is your heart established? Did I mention that HE'S COMING BACK!!??!!)

2 TIMOTHY 2:24 ESV

And the Lord's servant must not be quarrelsome but kind to everyone, able to teach, patiently enduring evil...
(Yes, it's evil out there. Are you still teaching and being kind anyway?)
JAMES 5:7 ESV
Be patient, therefore, brothers, until the coming of the Lord. See how the farmer waits for the precious fruit of the earth, being patient about it, until it receives the early and the late rains.
(Be patient, teach, let the Word grow and be constantly ready because HE IS COMING BACK!!!)

By the way, we finally made it to our house. But I'm looking forward to the last flight I'll ever take... when He comes back and I get to go home. I hope to see you there.

WEEK 13

Get Over The Hump Day WHAT I LOVE/HATE ABOUT EASTER Devotional:

"AND AFTER THE CRUCIFIXION THE DISCIPLES WENT ON AN EGG HUNT"

-said no one, ever

I won't make you wait for it. I hate egg hunts and new clothes on Easter. Maybe hate is a strong word. It's more of an attention-grabber. Have my children done egg hunts or gotten new clothes? Yes. Did I hunt eggs? Yes. Do I think my parents were wrong for letting me hunt eggs? No. Do I think those who hunt eggs are evil and missing the point? Uhm.....haha. No, I don't. I don't hate eggs, candy, or clothing. I will hide eggs for my kids anytime during the year, but not on Easter. I won't be attending anymore egg hunts, and I won't be hiding eggs on Easter. And I won't be out looking for a new dress either! Wait, I feel like that could be confusing....lol. I don't wear dresses. The last time I went to an egg hunt at a church helped solidify my position. It was GOOD FRIDAY, and all the kids lined up to pick up eggs at church. The church had broken the egg-hunting up into age groups. My son was about 7, and my daughter was in the older group at 9. Out in the field of a thousand eggs were 2 very large "prize eggs" for whoever could get there first. A lady in my church, who had two boys in this group, yelled, "GO GET'EM BOYS!" That is not made up. It really happened. When they said, "go," you would have thought there was a million dollars in those prize eggs, as kids crushed the other eggs under their feet trying to get out to those colorful, plastic, oblong holders of candy. I saw a little girl shoved down and almost trampled as kids raced to win. The same thing occurred with my daughter's age group, and I took my kids home and explained to them why we'd never ever go to the egg hunt at church again. This all happened... AT CHURCH! It seems it's getting harder to tell the church from the world, isn't it? Easter is all about the empty tomb and a risen Savior. We don't need anything else. That's how I feel about the eggs and clothing. Please don't think I have any ill feelings towards those who like to do the clothes or the eggs. I just can't make it fit in my life, and please don't agree with me too strongly either... as if I were trying to get people to stop. I'm just sharing where I am with it right now. So I pray you're not offended, and please keep reading because the real point is in the next paragraph. I'll just say this: Easter is about my Savior dying for me to bring Glory to Himself, and of course RISING FROM THE DEAD to accomplish that task! I'm through letting anything distract from that on Easter (or more adequately titled RESURRECTION SUNDAY.) I love thinking about The Story of Jesus on Easter. All of it. The Whole Story. How He came from heaven. How He lived while He was here. The way He taught. Him bleeding in the garden (more from that in a moment), being crucified, being buried, and rising from the dead. The details will never get old to me. We get out a tent and sit in it the night before Easter. It symbolizes the tomb where Jesus was buried. We read the story and find a detail to marvel about and then we zip up the tent. The next morning the tent is open, and it's empty. And it makes me happy. Sometimes we leave some of the sins we're struggling with inside the tent by writing them down the night before, and the kids watch them disappear overnight. No, I don't read the papers. That's between them and God... unless they want to share them with us. And no, I don't let them think it's some sort of magic. They know I take them out and throw them away, and they know I get up and open the tomb. It's the symbolism that we care about, and we feel it honors God. That's why we do it.

I just want to highlight one part of the story today. My favorite part is the garden. There HE IS in the garden. He's praying so intently that He's sweating drops of blood. And then He goes and hides some eggs for the disciples to find. Yeah, sounds silly doesn't it? I'm just saying. LOL. Sorry, back to the story. He's praying, "If possible please let this cup (punishment) pass, yet not My will, but Thy Will be done." Total submission to The Father. One thing Jesus had always known was being One with His Father. They ARE ONE. His concern here wasn't, I don't believe for a minute, a beating or being crucified. Hundreds of people had been beaten and crucified. I believe with my whole heart that what He didn't want was sin to be on Him and, mostly, to be separated from His Father. That is utter Hell. He's so concerned about being separated from God that He's literally sweating blood. What kills me is how we, as Christians, seem to think sin that separates us from our Father is not that big of a deal! A "little white lie"? Who came up with that crap? There are no "little" sins. One sin separates us from our Father. One sin. One sin made the devil who he is. One sin sends a soul into torment for all eternity. Yes, just one. Jesus had never ever sinned, and had never felt the hell of being separated from His Father. I would venture to say that if Christians were more concerned about where they are in their relationship with God The Father that we wouldn't have near the problems we have in the Christian community today. Our sin was the cause of the death of Jesus. So I'll never believe there's a "minor" one.

(LUKE 22:39-46 Jesus went out as usual to the Mount of Olives, and his disciples followed him. 40 On reaching the place, he said to them, "Pray that

you will not fall into temptation." 41 He
withdrew about a stone's throw beyond
them, knelt down and prayed, 42
"Father, if you are willing, take this cup
from me; yet not my will, but yours be
done." 43 An angel from heaven
appeared to him and strengthened him.
44 And being in anguish, he prayed
more earnestly, and his sweat was like
drops of blood falling to the ground. 45
When he rose from prayer and went
back to the disciples, he found them
asleep, exhausted from sorrow. 46 "Why
are you sleeping?" he asked them. "Get
up and pray so that you will not fall into
temptation.")

Take a moment. Be there in the garden with Jesus in your mind. Pray the end of that prayer. "Not my will, but Yours be done," and hate that sin in your life that keeps you from a more powerful and more precious walk with God. Don't sleepwalk through this life. Pray that you won't fall into that temptation to think sin is no big deal. Ask for His forgiveness and feel yourself being drawn nearer to Him already. If you will draw near to Him, He will draw near to you (JAMES 4:8). I believe in Jesus and that He died and rose again. I confess Him as Lord. You can too. Please do. HE IS Lord whether anyone confesses it this side of the judgement or not. I pray for those who don't believe...that they will believe, and that they won't experience that separation from God. Maybe you're reading this and you think that comedian dude is crazy for believing all that about Jesus. That's ok with me, I'm gonna believe in Him with all I am. I guess you could say, "I've put all my eggs in one basket."

WEEK 14

Get Over The Hump Day CHOOSE YOUR ATTITUDE Devotional:

Spring is a great time to get a fresh start on life... or not. Flowers and trees are blooming and causing bad allergies, birds are singing and pooping all over the place, squirrels are chattering and stealing all your bird food, the sun is out causing skin cancer, and the bees are buzzing and stinging folks. Ahh...it's a beautiful or irritating time of year, depending on what perspective you choose. I used to call myself a realist, which was my way of justifying my negativity. Is that you? If so, it's gotta change. I'm also a little skeptical of those people who are so happy all the time that they just don't seem real. I'm usually expecting them to try to sell me something. I'M LOOKING TO BE POSITIVE IN A VERY REAL WAY. I believe we, as Christians, should be real. I also believe we should be positive, which begins with a thankful heart. As a comedian I can promise you there are people out there who claim to be believers but have such a sour outlook on life that it seems they bathe in lemon juice every morning. There are people in every church who are always looking to be offended and need everyone to know how, when, and why they were offended. And while they may or may not be real believers, what we know for sure is that they sure don't look or act like true believers. Now, let's look in the mirror and make sure there's not a big log in our eye before we continue. If there is, take this time to remove it. I will do the same. Can everyone see now? Ok then, let's get serious about being real and positive. I keep saying real because some would have you believe that Christians are always happy, have no problems, and are just being blessed with so much material blessing they just can't handle it. A Godly positive attitude will never have anything to do with what material things you have, and it's basis is centered around the Joy of knowing Jesus. It's all about your walk with Jesus Christ. PERIOD. Let' s get seriously positive here today!

You should be displaying these attributes as a believer. Love, JOY, Peace, Patience, Kindness, Goodness, Faithfulness, Gentleness and Self-Control. (GALATIANS 5:22-23). Now, let's look at some scriptures to help us get motivated in the right direction today.

DEUTERONOMY 28:47-48 ESV

Because you did not serve the Lord your God with joyfulness and gladness of heart, because of the abundance of all things, therefore you shall serve your enemies whom the Lord will send against you, in hunger and thirst, in nakedness, and lacking everything. And he will put a yoke of iron on your neck until he has destroyed you.

-It seems the attitude of our hearts is important

MATTHEW 12:33 ESV

“Either make the tree good and its fruit good, or make the tree bad and its fruit bad, for the tree is known by its fruit.

-We will be known by our attitudes and actions we produce

EPHESIANS 4:31-32 ESV

Let ALL bitterness and wrath and anger and clamor and slander be put away from you, along with ALL malice. Be kind to one another, tenderhearted, forgiving one another, as God in Christ forgave you.

-Did you notice the word “all”?

EPHESIANS 4:29 ESV

Let no corrupting talk come out of your mouths, but only such as is good for building up, as fits the occasion, that it may give grace to those who hear.

-Does your attitude build up?

PHILIPPIANS 2:14 NASB

Do ALL things without grumbling or disputing

-There's that sneaky word "all" again....

PROVERBS 18:7 ESV

A fool's mouth is his ruin, and his lips are a snare to his soul.

-What is your mouth saying about you?

PROVERBS 15:1 ESV

A soft answer turns away wrath, but a harsh word stirs up anger.

-Let's be careful as we choose our words to go along with our joyful attitudes

1 THESSALONIANS 5:21 ESV

But test everything; hold fast what is good.

-Maybe that includes our attitude choices.

1 CORINTHIANS 10:31 ESV

So, whether you eat or drink, or whatever you do, do ALL to the glory of God.

-That word ALL keeps coming up!

OK LET'S GET THIS REFRESHED NEW JOYFUL ATTITUDE GOING NOW WITH THIS!!!!

ROMANS 12:2 ESV

Do not be conformed to this world, but be transformed by the renewal of your mind, that by testing you may discern what is the will of God, what is good and acceptable and perfect.

-Don't be normal, life's better than that

PSALM 19:14 ESV

Let the words of my mouth and the meditation of my heart be acceptable in your sight, O Lord, my rock and my redeemer.

-Are our attitudes acceptable in His sight?

COLOSSIANS 3:2 ESV

Set your minds on things that are above, not on things that are on earth.

-You choose what to set your mind on

PSALM 118:24 ESV

This is the day that the Lord has made; let us rejoice and be glad in it.
-You got another day!!
PROVERBS 17:22 ESV
A joyful heart is good medicine, but a crushed spirit dries up the bones.
-Take that medicine and give it out at work today!!
PROVERBS 15:13 ESV
A glad heart makes a cheerful face, but by sorrow of heart the spirit is crushed.
-Let me see that cheerful face!!
1 THESSALONIANS 5:16-18 ESV
Rejoice always, pray without ceasing, give thanks in ALL circumstances; for this is the will of God in Christ Jesus for you.
-ALWAYS REJOICE IN “ALL” CIRCUMSTANCES
AND
PHILIPPIANS 4:8 ESV
Finally, brothers, whatever is true, whatever is honorable, whatever is just, whatever is pure, whatever is lovely, whatever is commendable, if there is any excellence, if there is anything

worthy of praise, think about these things.

It's time to refresh. Let's see the sun and birds and trees as beautiful things. Let's look around and choose joyful attitudes. Let's honor God as we choose thankfulness over those other attitudes that come so easily to us (sadness, bitterness, annoyance, complaining, etc.). You can make a difference in someone's life today! I'm serious. You truly can, and all it takes is choosing an attitude.

I'm recommending a book to you today that has helped me tremendously. It's called, Lord, Change My Attitude (Before It's Too Late) by James MacDonald. Enjoy this day!!

WEEK 15

Get Over The Hump Day TAXES Devotional:

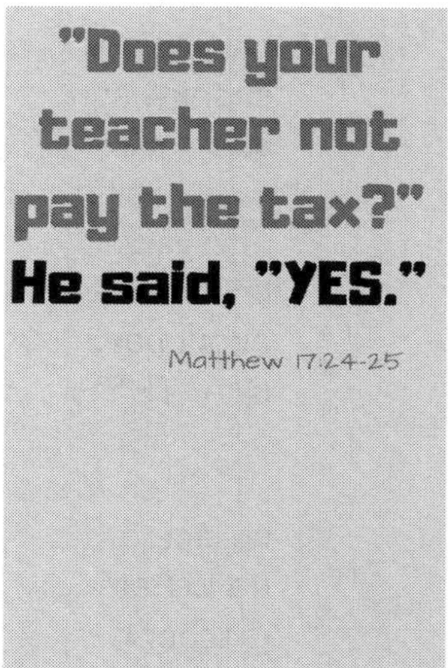

Paying taxes is, well....taxing. Hahahaha. Ok, it wasn't that funny. I've always thought the paying of taxes was a pretty mean trick on the government's part. Here's why. I've been to 16 years of school and graduated first in my class (alphabetically), and double-majored in college. And not once, Never, Ever,

Ever, and I mean NEVER, was I ever, in all those years of school, once made to learn about paying taxes. Not one class, not one semester, not one hour of tax class. Folks, something is really pretty sneaky, strange, or just downright wrong about that, right? Of course there's something wrong with it, but I think it's always been that way. Feelings aside, let's read about what the Bible says about paying taxes.

(MATTHEW 17:24-27 ESV)

The Temple Tax

24 When they came to Capernaum, the
collectors of the two-drachma tax went
up to Peter and said, "Does your
teacher not pay the tax?" 25 He said,
"Yes." And when he came into the
house, Jesus spoke to him first, saying,
"What do you think, Simon? From whom
do kings of the earth take toll or tax?
From their sons or from others?" 26 And
when he said, "From others," Jesus said
to him, "Then the sons are free.
27 However, not to give offense to them,
go to the sea and cast a hook and take
the first fish that comes up, and when

you open its mouth you will find a shekel. Take that and give it to them for me and for yourself."

Soooo apparently even if you're The One that created the entire universe, the government will still expect you to pay taxes.

This is one of the many wonderful and comical stories in the Bible. There are soooo many things to draw from in how he got the tax. You know the tax collectors had to be standing there waiting on the payment when Peter went and grabbed his fishing pole. Did they watch him do this? Did he whistle the theme to The Andy Griffith Show on the way? He catches a fish and takes the money out of its mouth and hands it to them. That's awesome and hilarious. I just want to see their faces. You know they talked about that for the rest of their tax collecting days! "Dude, you remember when that guy caught that fish and got the money out of its mouth?" "Uh, do I remember? I took up fishing the next day..." And I love that he had Peter get the tax by doing what he did for a living.

There's so many reasons to be annoyed with the government. There's a thousand reasons to want to not pay them or to cheat on your taxes. I know it's a temptation for thousands of people each year, but it has no place in the life of a Christian. Jesus owns it all, and of course He didn't need to pay taxes. However, He set the example for us to follow and so my check is in the mail. I'm going to pay my taxes. I'm going to pay quarterly taxes. Now, if I can only choose a good attitude about it, I'll be on my way to being more like Jesus. Baby steps, right? It doesn't really matter what the government does or doesn't do. It really only matters what God teaches us to do. So let's do our part to set a good example, and if the IRS comes knocking at your door just take them down to the lake and go fishing. Tell them the story of Jesus and Peter, and hand them a fish. And it'd be cool if somehow you could sneak your check into it's mouth and pull it out and hand it to them like a magician does the whole quarter-out-of-the-ear thing. That would be epic. (If you ever do this, put it on Youtube so we can watch it.)

There's another point to that story. It's that God is still in control. He had a fish eat a coin, swim around and wait for Peter to throw in his line, and then bite that line. He calms the seas and He sometimes allows donkeys to talk (insert government joke here). No matter what we think about our government, it will always be in a state of change. So let's keep our focus on The One who never changes. Paying taxes isn't us giving to the government. It's us bowing low and worshipping our God and saying to Him, "I love You, therefore I will honor You by Obeying You." That is what changes my attitude when I consider paying taxes. I want to make My Father proud. Now go pay those taxes, and then take the day off and go fishing. Hey, you never know. There might be a refund check in the next one you catch!

WEEK 16

Get Over The Hump Day ZOMBIES AND ALIENS Devotional:

I believe there are aliens and zombies. I just don't believe they exist the way that they are portrayed on television and the movies. Hear me out. The way zombies are described is basically that they are, as the popular

TV show is titled, “The Walking Dead.” I certainly don’t think we need to watch the show to get the point. As I understand the idea, it goes something like this: The people are dead and walking around simply filling their appetites with whatever they happen to walk across, and they’ll do anything to get it. They are a danger and are constantly trying to drag down the living and destroy them. To survive, apparently, you just have to stay away from them and remain unbitten. And to destroy them you must kill the brain. I’m sure there’s more to the story, but that’s the basic idea.

Aliens, on the other hand, have been portrayed for years as some mysterious creatures that we, as earthlings, are on the lookout for. And we should be prepared to fight against their takeover. In almost every movie, television show, and story book, the humans somehow destroy these aliens (who were surely here to destroy us). Although they were more advanced and more intelligent, we perceived their threat to us and were somehow able to destroy them before they destroyed us.

Both of these scenarios are fictitious....but also very real. Let me paint a picture for you. We live in a world where spiritually dead people are walking around every day trying to fill their appetites with anything and everything they happen to stumble across. The earth is overrun with such people, and they would love nothing more than for you to become like them. They need to be revived before they are destroyed. Yes, there is a cure. The Gospel is the cure. There is a judgment coming, and time is limited. The Lord of All Light came into the world and died for the sins of us all, so that those who would believe in Him would be saved (JOHN 3:16) and turned from death to life. Those of us who belong to Him and have given our lives to Him are aliens in this world. Our home is in another land. A land that is filled with The Glory of God, The Father of Light. We do not belong here, and we're trying to spread that news to all who will listen. But the world is deceived into thinking that these aliens are here to destroy THEM and THEIR way of life. When the reality is that we have come to tell them that they can have true life and have it more abundantly. It is a war. The brain must be infused with the truth of the word of God, and it will move the heart as God speaks. God will save them, if they will listen. And He has charged us with the task of sharing the truth with them. Through that truth the dead can be regenerated. Think I'm crazy yet? Well, I am. But here's some scripture to think about today:

EPHESIANS 2:1-7

And YOU WERE DEAD in your trespasses and sins, in which you formerly walked according to the course of this world, according to the prince of the power of the air, of the spirit that is now working in the sons of disobedience. Among them we too all formerly lived in the lusts of our flesh, indulging the desires of the flesh and of the mind, and were by nature children of wrath, even as the rest. But God, being rich in mercy, because of His great love with which He loved us, even when WE WERE DEAD in our transgressions, made us alive together with Christ (by grace you have been saved), and raised us up with Him, and seated us with Him in the heavenly places in Christ Jesus, so that in the ages to come He might show the surpassing riches of His grace in kindness toward us in Christ Jesus. (JESUS CHRIST IS OUR HERO)

<u>ROMANS 5:12;18</u>

12 Therefore, just as through one man sin entered into the world, and death through sin, and so DEATH SPREAD TO ALL MEN, because all sinned—

18 So then as through one transgression there resulted condemnation to all men, even so through one act of righteousness there resulted justification of life to all men. (JESUS WAS/IS POWERFUL ENOUGH TO REVERSE THE CURSE AND COME TO OUR RESCUE)

<u>COLOSSIANS 2:8-15</u>

See to it that no one takes you captive through philosophy and empty deception, according to the tradition of men, according to the elementary principles of the world, rather than according to Christ. For in Him all the fullness of Deity dwells in bodily form, and IN HIM YOU HAVE BEEN MADE COMPLETE, and He is the head over all rule and authority; and in Him you were also circumcised with a circumcision made without hands, in the removal of the body of the flesh by the circumcision of Christ; having been buried with Him in baptism, in which you were also raised up with Him through faith in the working of God, who raised Him from the dead. When YOU WERE DEAD in your transgressions and the uncircumcision of your flesh, HE MADE YOU ALIVE together with Him, having forgiven us all our transgressions, having canceled out the certificate of debt consisting of decrees against us, which was hostile to us; and He has taken it out of the way, having nailed it to the cross. When He had disarmed the rulers and authorities, He made a public display of them, having triumphed over them through

Him. (JESUS CHRIST DEFEATED THE ENEMY SO THAT YOU COULD BE SAVED)

GALATIANS 5:13-24

For you were called to freedom, brethren; only do not turn your freedom into an opportunity for the flesh, but through love serve one another. For the whole Law is fulfilled in one word, in the statement, “You shall love your neighbor as yourself.” But if you bite and devour one another, take care that you are not consumed by one another.

But I say, WALK BY THE SPIRIT AND YOU WILL NOT CARRY OUT THE DESIRE OF THE FLESH. For the flesh sets its desire against the Spirit, and the Spirit against the flesh; for these are in opposition to one another, so that you may not do the things that you please. But if you are led by the Spirit, you are not under the Law. Now the deeds of the flesh are evident, which are: immorality, impurity, sensuality, idolatry, sorcery, enmities, strife, jealousy, outbursts of anger, disputes, dissensions, factions, envying, drunkenness, carousing, and things like these, of which I forewarn you, just as I have forewarned you, that those who practice such things will not inherit the kingdom of God. But the fruit of the Spirit is love, joy, peace, patience, kindness, goodness, faithfulness, gentleness, self-control; against such things there is no law. Now those who belong to Christ Jesus have crucified the flesh with its passions and desires. (THE SPIRIT PRODUCES FRUIT IN THOSE WHO ARE TRANSFORMED FROM DEATH TO LIFE).

So we are a band of brothers and sisters out there, as aliens, with instructions from our leader that we are to save as many people as we can through the spreading of the gospel that can regenerate souls, and take as many people to heaven with us as possible. For this is not our home:

<u>1 PETER 2:11</u>

Beloved, I urge you as ALIENS AND STRANGERS to abstain from fleshly lusts which wage war against the soul.

<u>HEBREWS 11:13-16</u>

All these died in faith, without receiving the promises, but having seen them and having welcomed them from a distance, and having confessed that they were STRANGERS AND EXILES ON THE EARTH. For those who say such things make it clear that they are seeking a country of their own. And indeed if they had been thinking of that country from which they went out, they would have had opportunity to return

PHILIPPIANS 3:20

For OUR CITIZENSHIP IS IN HEAVEN, from which also we eagerly wait for a Savior, the Lord Jesus Christ;

JOHN 17:16

"THEY ARE NOT OF THE WORLD, even as I am not of the world."

JOHN 15:18-19

"If the world hates you, you know that it has hated Me before it hated you. "If you were of the world, the world would love its own; but because YOU ARE NOT OF THE WORLD, but I chose you out of the world, because of this the world hates you.

We're just passing through, so hold on loosely to things here on this earth and focus on bringing the dead to life with the message of the gospel. Then we'll be able to take as many with us as possible when our Savior comes and takes us home. Don't live like a zombie. Live like an alien in this world always longing for the day when you will get to go back home. Set your mind on the things above (COLOSSIANS 3:2). Let's bring life to the dead today!!!

WEEK 17

Get Over The Hump Day HUGE BATHROOM Devotional:

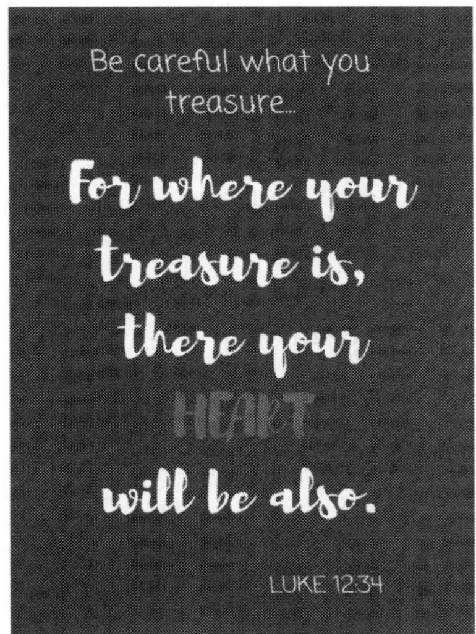

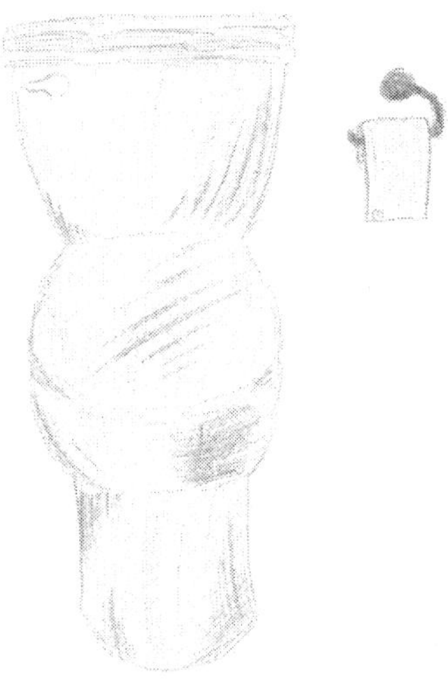

Bradley and I were in a hurry to make it to a show close to home. We were in a hurry because we had just flown in from out of town and had gotten our car from the airport and were speeding along to make it on time. It was a corporate party for a company that was being held at someones home. We had been on a plane and getting our bags and our car and hitting the road to make it on time, so I hadn't had time to go to the bathroom. We finally pull up to the house, and the man is there waiting on us. He's very energetic and excited about showing us this home. All I could think about was needing to "go." As it so happened the thing he was most excited about showing us was this enormous bathroom. He took us upstairs and, while pointing things out to the left and right, he was headed straight for what he was apparently most proud of.....the bathroom. We finally arrived and it was indeed impressive...and pretty ridiculous. There was a TV mounted up by the shower so you could watch while you lathered, an impressive tub in case you wanted to relax and watch the game whilst in the midst of bubbles, and a gorgeous sink area so you could beautify yourself with the largest mirror possible. And most importantly there was what I needed.....finally.....a toilet! All I needed was for them to leave me alone in there for about a minute, and I could be at ease and maybe even take interest in what he was showing us. Finally he directed us to move on, and that's when I said, "Hey can I use the bathroom?" And without missing a beat, he just said, "No, now let me show you downstairs." It was a weirdly funny moment. I immediately began laughing to myself, and once we got downstairs and he started showing us the sound system, I asked if there was a bathroom that I could use before we started checking the sound. He directed me to a small restroom in the hallway, and as I finally got the relief I needed, I started laughing out loud there in that tiny restroom. You just can't make this stuff up. Here was this guy so proud of his bathroom and how immaculate it was and all that he'd put into it, but it was just for him to use and to show other people what he'd done.....for himself. It was a nice bathroom, but it was useless to me and the rest of the world.

The point is that we don't want to be this way as Christians. What good is telling people all about your church, your Bible study group, or even your Savior if they can't see or be invited to have what you have? We can't simply show others around the faith. We must be examples of how to live it and how to use it. Let's take a moment and do a quick assessment of our lives. This is probably a good idea to do on a regular basis. For this assessment, and all others, let's always use Scripture. (LUKE 12:34 For where your treasure is, there your heart will be also.)

Maybe your treasure is in your bathroom too. Let's try to think on a higher plane shall we? If you've got a great bathroom, and you want to show it off, maybe at least let someone else use it! Ok, it's fine to have a great bathroom but let's strive to set up treasure for ourselves in heaven by serving God and doing good to others.

(JAMES 1:22-25 But prove yourselves doers of the word, and not merely hearers who delude themselves. For if anyone is a hearer of the word and not a doer, he is like a man who looks at his natural face in a mirror (maybe even a real big huge impressive new mirror); for once he has looked at himself and gone away, he has immediately forgotten what kind of person he was. But one who looks intently at the perfect law, the law of liberty, and abides by it, not having become a forgetful hearer but an effectual doer, this man will be blessed in what he does.)

Are you one of those hearers only? I don't think God has any intentions of changing hearts and lives just so people will sit at home and do nothing. I'm pretty sure if you have the means to build an incredible bathroom, then maybe you could also have the heart to share it or even build someone else one. The point is, do something. Today. For someone else.

(MATTHEW 7:12 Do unto others as you would have them do unto you.......)

That's pretty self explanatory. If you would want others to let you use their bathroom when you have to go, then you should also allow others to use your bathroom when they have to go.

Am I harping too much on this bathroom thing?
Here's the verse I really want to focus on today. Hopefully you will too: (PHILIPPIANS 2:3-4 ESV Do nothing from rivalry or conceit, but in humility count others more significant than yourselves. Let each of you look not only to his own interests, but also to the interests of others.)

There's never anything we can say as well as Scripture says it. This is God speaking. It's healthy to remember in the midst of this world that life isn't about us. I know everyone says it is. The world is teaching us to get all we can, can all we get, and then sit on our cans (on an immaculate can if we can afford it). But that's not the believer's lifestyle at all. We are to be looking out for the good of others, being humble and counting others as better than ourselves. Obviously that doesn't mean belittling ourselves. It means to really, genuinely, and sincerely CARE ABOUT OTHERS DEEPLY. We live in a world that is building huge bathrooms for themselves, and they want to show others what they have. Let's be believers who share about another world where there is a God who cares and is building something grand for us all. (And thankfully He's building us more than just a bathroom). Let's share the love of Christ with others. Build whatever you're going to build, but try to build it with the purpose of blessing others.

Now go out there and invite someone over to use your bathroom!

WEEK 18

Get Over The Hump Day "GOD HELPS THOSE WHO HELP THEMSELVES" Devotional:

There's nothing like hearing those words, "Help yourself," because that usually means I'm about to get a piece of candy or a cookie or some other wonderful treat. I learned that as a kid. When you see candy at Granny's house, she's gonna say those magical words, "Help yourself." While we're speaking about helping ourselves... Have you noticed there are self-help books in the bookstores and libraries? I believe they even have their own section. In so many ways we can help ourselves and should continue to strive to make ourselves better each day. That wood isn't gonna chop itself...somebody has to pick up the axe, right? There's the axe, "help yourself" and you can be warm. These are all concepts I understand and have heard since I was a child. As I grew, I also heard this phrase a lot: "God helps those who help themselves." I never heard it at home, but I did hear it often in passing from teachers at school etc. Then finally one day, I was working with a friend and we were riding in his truck. I forget what we were talking about, but I remember him saying, "You know what the Bible says...God helps those who help themselves..." And for the first time it hit me that I was pretty sure the Bible DOESN'T say that, and how wrong and pretty ridiculous that phrase actually is considering what the Bible DOES teach.

When it comes to helping ourselves, we definitely need to do so when chopping wood. Or else it will just sit there and that fire won't build itself. We definitely want to help ourselves when invited to eat a cookie...especially if it's chocolate chip. But when it comes to salvation, we are utterly helpless and totally incapable of helping ourselves. (EPHESIANS 2:1 And you were dead in your trespasses and sins..). Dead people can't help themselves to salvation. In fact, no one has the ability to even know they need help without the Father drawing us to Himself (JOHN 6:44 "No one can come to Me unless the Father who sent Me draws him; and I will raise him up on the last day.) And then there's the whole "camel through the eye of a needle" saying that teaches us that with men, salvation is impossible, but praise the Lord it is possible through HIM (LUKE 18).

That phrase seems like a wise thing to say, but in some contexts it is actually foolish. And it is not at all in the Bible. Yes, some folks in The White House have "quoted it" from the Bible. But it's not in there, and probably sheds a little light on how much our government officials read the Bible.

We need to understand that there are times in life that we can in no way help ourselves and need The Holy Spirit to be our great helper. He has promised He will help those who can NOT help themselves. Here are some good examples in scripture:

(ISAIAH 25:4 For You have been a defense for the HELPLESS,
A defense for the needy in his distress,
A refuge from the storm, a shade from the heat...)
(ROMANS 5:6 For while we were still HELPLESS, at the right time Christ died for the ungodly.)
(JOHN 15:5 "I am the vine, you are the branches; he who abides in Me and I in him, he bears much fruit, for APART FROM ME, YOU CAN DO NOTHING.)

Listen up, my brothers and sisters. I just want to remind you that you are not left alone, expected to be doing things by yourself. While we must take responsibility and take action, we also must guard against any idea that isn't Scriptural. God doesn't sit back and wait to see how much you're helping yourself before He will come to your aid. We do need to be working out our salvation (PHILIPPIANS 2:12-13 So then, my beloved, just as you have always obeyed, not as in my presence only, but now much more in my absence, work out your salvation with fear and trembling; for it is God who is at work in you, both to will and to work for His good pleasure). But it can't be done without God's help. Some things are too much for us to take on, and the good news is that God helps those who CAN'T help themselves... those who have no control over situations in this life, and those who are weary and worn. Lean on Him. He will help you get through each and every circumstance.

Now go help yourself to a cookie.

WEEK 19

Get Over The Hump Day "GOD NEVER GIVES YOU MORE THAN YOU CAN BEAR" Devotional:

Cancer seems to be everywhere. Countless godly people have lost their loved ones to this disease. People are racked with loss, and a story just came on the news about a family that lost their children in a car wreck. I think of three of my friends that died way too young to a car wreck, a suicide, and an accidental overdose. And I think of the difficulty of losing my mother when I was a boy, and how hard that was for my father in those days trying to deal with that and take care of his two boys. As I think of all of that, I think how silly some of these phrases are that we hear over and over again.

Let's take on a popular phrase that people THINK is in The Bible, but is NOT. That phrase being, "God never gives you more than you can handle." I contend that every example I gave above is far too much for anyone to handle. I won't pretend that I would be able to handle any of those above circumstances. Furthermore, if you're going through some terrible circumstance, please take this time to feel relieved that The Bible does not expect you to be able to handle these things alone.

Here is where we get that idea from: <u>1 CORINTHIANS 10:12-13</u> Therefore let him who thinks he stands take heed that he does not fall. 13 NO

TEMPTATION HAS OVERTAKEN YOU BUT SUCH AS IS COMMON TO MAN; AND GOD IS FAITHFUL, WHO WILL NOT ALLOW YOU TO BE TEMPTED BEYOND WHAT YOU ARE ABLE, but with the temptation will provide the way of escape also, so that you will be able to endure it.

Folks, that verse is about temptation to sin. Sin is impossible to bear. Hence the need for a Savior to die for our sins. Now, falling to the temptation to sin can be avoided, because God won't allow you to be tempted beyond what you can bear. Because with every temptation He will provide a way out. This, of course, has nothing to do with bearing terrible burdens that come our way. It's great news to know that we can overcome temptation with God's help. But we're talking today about bearing difficulties. So let's get back to the point with a verse from The Bible.

2 CORINTHIANS 1:8 For we do not want you to be unaware, brethren, of our affliction which came to us in Asia,

that we were burdened excessively, BEYOND OUR STRENGTH, so that we despaired even of life...

The first few verses of 2 Corinthians explain a little bit of why we go through life's struggles: 2 CORINTHIANS 1:3-4

3 Blessed be the God and Father of our Lord Jesus Christ, the Father of mercies and God of all comfort, 4 who comforts us in all our affliction so that we will be able to comfort those who are in any affliction with the comfort with which we ourselves are comforted by God.

We don't have to bear our burdens alone. Our source of strength is Jesus Christ, and He expects us to help bear one another's burdens. (GALATIANS 6:2 - Bear one another's burdens, and so fulfill the law of Christ.)

If you're struggling, you're in good company:

PSALMS 38:4 For my iniquities have gone over my head;

like a heavy burden, they are too heavy for me.

1 KINGS 19:7-8 And the angel of the Lord came again a second time and touched him (Elijah) and said, "Arise and eat, for THE JOURNEY IS TOO GREAT FOR YOU." 8 And he arose and ate and drank, and went in the strength of that food forty days and forty nights to Horeb, the mount of God.

So rest assured that God is with you today. His plan is for us to help each other through these difficult times. He has promised to work things out for good to those that love Him (ROMANS 8:28). He does have a purpose. I get the privilege of hearing incredible stories of the revival that went on during my mom's sickness that led to her death. I get the joy of knowing the mother that He sent to us after my birth mother passed on. I get the joy of having two families, instead of just one to love. And I still hear wonderful stories of what a godly woman my mother was, and I get to see what a godly woman my mother now is. And her story is amazing too, as she came to us in the midst of losing her fiancé. That story is for a different time.

The point is that burdens may come that are too much for you to bear alone. Don't ever feel like you're supposed to handle them alone. Pick up the phone. Christians be ready to love and support your brothers and sisters in their time of need.

Thank you God that you never give us more than YOU can handle.

WEEK 20

Get Over The Hump Day
GRADUATION Devotional:

Graduation is a special time. I'll never forget graduating high school. I was standing in line with my friends, and I noticed that some of them had something written on the outside of the paper we were supposed to hand to the person reading off our names. I asked what it was, and they explained to me that it said "Tennessee Honors." They informed me what it took to get that honor, and I felt that I had done enough to get it myself. So I wrote it on my piece of paper as well. When it came my turn, I handed it to the guy reading the names as I walked across the stage, and my parents were shocked to find out that I had graduated with "Tennessee Honors." I imagine my teachers were also kind of surprised. Apparently, sometimes to get an honor all you have to do is write it down on a piece of paper!

Frankly, after looking back, for many people all graduation ends up being is just another piece of paper with their name on it. I'm challenging you today to make your graduation day mean so much more. When I look back, I remember friends that I made, things that I did, and places I went. Most importantly, I remember loving people. Clearly I wasn't perfect in any phase of school, but I always had a love for people. That is what I still carry with me today. The graduation certificate doesn't mean much anymore, but the people I got to know throughout middle school, high school, and college... and still pray for through all these years... makes all the difference. I was far from being an evangelist, but as far back as I can remember I did care about people and their salvation. I certainly didn't personally witness to all my friends, but I did witness to some and still pray for others. I know I needed people praying for me, and it certainly wouldn't have been hard for someone to find a mistake I'd made or some sin in my own life. But the fact that God gave me a love for people made my school days worth so much more than just the paper I got saying I was there. I hope that if you're still in school that you will develop a genuine love for others. Influence people with your encouragement, and let them see your light shine (MATTHEW 5:16 - In the same way, let your light shine before others, so that they may see your good works and give glory to your Father who is in heaven.)

Pray for those God lays on your heart. If your schooling is done and you're out there in the work place, the challenge is still the same. LOVE OTHERS.
(MATTHEW 22:37-39 "Love the Lord your God with all your heart and with all your soul and with all your mind.' This is the first and greatest
commandment. And the second is like it: 'Love your neighbor as yourself."
JOHN 13:34-35 "A new command I give you: Love one another. As I have loved you, so you must love one another. By this everyone will know that you are my disciples, if you love one another."
ROMANS 12:10 "Be devoted to one another in love. Honor one another above yourselves."
1 JOHN 4:7-8 "Dear friends, let us love one another, for love comes from God. Everyone who loves has been born of God and knows God. Whoever does not love does not know God, because God is love.")

I believe loving others makes living this life here worth it. No amount of awards, so-called achievements, money, fame, or things will make this life worthwhile. Loving others will make it all worth it. It helps life make sense. You're not done here. We're all still in school, in a way, because one day we will all graduate one last time. When we die we will pass on to the next life. That is the graduation that I'm looking forward to and the one in which I'd love to receive honors. I have no delusions that I will graduate at the top of my class, but I cant wait to take part in that ceremony when the King of all Kings and the Lord of all Lords calls out my name, and I stand before Him and He says to me, "Well done" (MATTHEW 25:21 - "His master replied, 'Well done, good and faithful servant! You have been faithful with a few things; I will put you in charge of many things. Come and share your master's happiness!'). That, and that alone, will make every second here on earth worth it. I know I can't EARN that honor. I can't sneak that one by Him.

Nothing gets past Him. My friends, I want nothing more in this life than to know that whoever may read this devotional today will take part in that final graduation ceremony with me. You can't EARN this graduation. You'll never deserve it. You can't buy it. Dying without it would be the greatest tragedy ever known. But you can take part in it, for free. You just ask for it. (ROMANS 10:8-10 But what does it say? "THE WORD IS NEAR YOU, IN YOUR MOUTH AND IN YOUR HEART"—that is, the word of faith which we are preaching, that if you confess with your mouth Jesus as Lord, and believe in your heart that God raised Him from the dead, you will be saved; for with the heart a person believes, resulting in righteousness, and with the mouth he confesses, resulting in salvation.) Ask God to reveal Himself to you today. Find out how knowing God can make this life worth more than you ever imagined. Discover how loving people can give you purpose. Find out that when you live for Him here, He will reward you when you get there.

Yes, there is one last graduation ceremony before it's all said and done. I want you all to receive that opportunity to graduate. Unfortunately, not everyone will. Let's love others and share this truth so they can graduate too......maybe even "with Tennessee Honors!"

<u>WEEK 21</u>

Get Over The Hump Day WHY IT FEELS LIKE GOD HAS FAILED YOU Devotional:

HE SAID TO THEM,
"BECAUSE OF YOUR LITTLE FAITH. FOR TRULY, I SAY TO YOU, IF YOU HAVE FAITH LIKE A GRAIN OF MUSTARD SEED, YOU WILL SAY TO THIS MOUNTAIN, 'MOVE FROM HERE TO THERE,' AND IT WILL MOVE, AND NOTHING WILL BE IMPOSSIBLE FOR YOU."

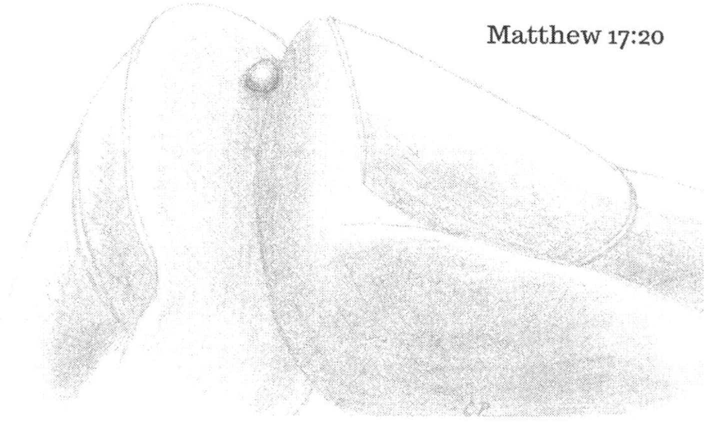

When I was about 8 years old I read this verse: <u>MATTHEW 17:20</u> He replied, "Because you have so little faith. Truly I tell you, if you have faith as small as a mustard seed, you can say to this mountain, 'Move from here to there,' and it will move. Nothing will be impossible for you." I was at church and I was standing on the softball field by myself looking out at the mountains. I believed that God was able to do what He said, and so I began to tell the mountains to move. I stood there and prayed in my heart and in my head and watched those mountains just stand there. No movement, none at all. I began to wonder if I lacked the faith of a tiny seed, or if God just wasn't hearing my prayers. I never doubted that God could move the mountain, but I certainly wondered why He didn't. God had failed me, or I had failed Him by having too little faith. Fast forward to college on a mission trip in Chattanooga, TN. We went to have breakfast with a group of widows. They would meet and have prayer together. This little woman began to pray, and as she prayed she began to say, "God I'm not asking You to move these mountains, I'm just asking for the strength to climb." I've never forgotten that prayer. Since that day I've often asked The Lord for the strength to climb. Here's why I think we feel God has failed us so many times.

I've lost loved ones unexpectedly, I've had many lost job opportunities throughout the years. I've had many big opportunities that I'd prayed for that didn't work out, and some that just came to me that I wasn't even looking for... and I got excited about them and they ended up falling through. I've talked with some pretty big name people in the Christian music world that gave me advice and made some promises that never came to fruition. I've hoped and prayed for things that I've never gotten, and I've struggled to pay off debts even though I felt I'd made wise decisions. I've prayed for things for others that didn't work out the way I wanted them to work out, and I've asked God what seems like a million times to send me guidance and felt like I didn't get an answer. Not to mention needing friends at times when there wasn't one to be found. God had failed me over and over and over again. That is, if He promised to give me everything that I asked for right when I asked for it and to get me what I wanted to make me happy. If that is what He promised, then He did indeed fail me at times. But rest assured He never promised us that we'd get what we wanted, when we wanted it. As a matter of fact when you look it over it sure seems He has some spoiled kids, doesn't it? I'll go even further to say that I don't find anywhere in The Bible where He promises that we'll be "happy" all the time here on this earth. I won't elaborate on that right now. I'm going to try to stick to this one point. Why does it "seem" that God is failing us?

I think the disappointment comes because we know and understand that God is just that...GOD. He owns everything, He controls everything, He is in charge. Nothing is too difficult for God. There's no amount of money that He can't provide, there's no amount of healing that is too hard for Him, and there's no situation that He can't fix. We read about Jesus walking the earth and touching and healing and providing for the needs of others. Calming storms, healing sickness, creating food, walking on water, even raising the dead! Then why can't He see that I need work, or that my friend needs healing?!? Maybe we have missed the point. Maybe this life is really all about the next life. Maybe we need to look beyond what we want when we're praying and ask God to reveal to us what we need to be praying for. Or maybe we are spoiled, selfish children, and when we don't get what we want we feel God has failed us. That sounds harsh but is probably true in many circumstances. Even if that is the case, rest assured that God is not tired of hearing your prayers. He loves you. He's patient and kind and He wants to hear you pray. He is listening to His children. We are imperfect, and we're imperfect parents. But He is not. He is perfect and long suffering, and no matter how we "feel" He will never, and has never, let us down. He's not mad at us because we're mad at Him. He doesn't walk away when you yell at Him. He doesn't hate that thing about you that you may hate or your spouse may complain about. He loves you perfectly. That is why He doesn't give us what we want, when we want it. This life is all about the next one. Listen to Him as He tries to tell us that. (ROMANS 14:7-8 For not one of us lives for himself, and not one dies for himself; for if we live, WE LIVE FOR THE LORD, or if we die, we die for the Lord; therefore whether we live or die, we are the Lord's).

Faith is more than moving mountains. It's trusting He will give you the strength to climb (HEBREWS 11:1, "Now faith is the substance of things hoped for, the evidence of things NOT SEEN.") This thing called "faith" has substance to it, but it can't be seen or always felt. It must be believed with your head and your heart. It is not blind. It is solid because it comes from trusting God's word.

Sometimes this life gets hard, but that's so we'll gain what we really need. (ROMANS 5:1-5 Therefore, having been justified by faith, we have peace with God through our Lord Jesus Christ, through whom also we have obtained our introduction by faith into this grace in which we stand; and we exult in hope of the glory of God. And not only this, but we also exult in our tribulations, knowing that TRIBULATION BRINGS ABOUT PERSEVERANCE; AND PERSEVERANCE, PROVEN CHARACTER; AND PROVEN CHARACTER, HOPE; and hope does not disappoint, because the love of God has been poured out within our hearts through the Holy Spirit who was given to us.).

God has never failed me. It sure feels like He has sometimes. I can still think of times that I feel like He let me down. Yep, it's true. Even now as I write this I can think of moments in my life that I don't understand and that I "feel" like He let me down. Whew, it feels good to be honest about that, doesn't it? Here's the thing: It doesn't matter how I "feel." It only matters what is true. I can feel like 2+2 equals 6 all I want, but it will always be 4. There will be times we may feel God has let us down, but let me assure you He hasn't. He loves you. He will never let you down. Look at Him hanging on that cross and remember that God loved you so much that He sent His own Son to die so that you could know Him and be known by Him. He won't withhold what is good for you. (JOHN 3:16)

The TRUTH is He has never failed us. HEBREWS 13:5 Make sure that your character is free from the love of money, being content with what you have; for He Himself has said, "I WILL NEVER DESERT YOU, NOR WILL I EVER FORSAKE YOU,"). I hope you feel loved when you read that, but even if you don't feel it, that's ok. It's still true. Believe it, and maybe your feelings will catch up with the truth.

WEEK 22

Get Over The Hump Day AT THE BEACH WHEN IT'S RAINING Devotional:

I'm at the beach right now and it's cold and rainy. That's the bad news. The great news is that we're with awesome friends, so we're having fun. That said, the point is when someone packs to go to the beach, what they are expecting is warm weather, sand, sun, etc. It's like traveling all the way across the country to get to Disney World or Wally World just to find out that it's closed for the month. Something about "rain on your wedding day, or a free ride when you've already paid" comes to mind. What I'm saying is that we can all tell when something has a purpose and that purpose is not being met. If you pack and go to the beach, you assume the purpose of the beach is sand and sun and fun. The purpose of Disney is to spend hours in line meeting mice and princesses, and the purpose of Wally World.....well, Marty Moose and roller coasters of course.

I guess what I'm saying is that Christians also have a purpose, and it becomes painfully evident when a believer is not fulfilling that purpose. For example...Christians that are always complaining, gossiping, or working for the purpose of making more and more money. Or missing out on time with the family when you don't have to just to make a little more green. There are thousands of examples and I'm not trying to point fingers. What I'd like to be doing is shedding light so someone might read this and simply think and pray something like this: "God am I fulfilling the purpose you have for me, or am I just living day to day with no real purpose?" Don't you want to be in the sand and sun when you're at the beach? Do you expect Disney to be closed when you get there with no warning at all? Let's take seriously our part in this walk of life. Let's remember today that WE HAVE A PURPOSE. We should be salt and light (MATTHEW 5:13-16 (NASB) "YOU ARE THE SALT OF THE EARTH; but if the salt has become tasteless, how can it be made salty again? It is no longer good for anything, except to be thrown out and trampled under foot by men. "YOU ARE THE LIGHT OF THE WORLD. A city set on a hill cannot be hidden; nor does anyone light a lamp and put it under a basket, but on the lamp stand, and it gives light to all who are in the house.

Let your light shine before men in such a way that they may see your good works, and glorify your Father who is in heaven.)

There is something expected of us as believers. Truth should burst forth from us unashamedly, mixed with the joy and love that flows from the heart of one who has been loved and redeemed by a Savior who conquered hell when He died for us. Correction falls from our lips, dripping with the empathy and understanding that it could and might someday be us needing the same correction. Love comes out of us with a humility only someone who has been saved from drowning in the sea of sin could understand. Loyalty is clear. Jesus is The One and Only and whose approval we seek and need. We are all different, but we're all in the same boat, with the same agenda and the same Savior. Once you've been pulled from the water, you're more aware of the dangers. And so you watch for others who are struggling to keep from drowning in the same sea of sin you were once in, and you're trying to throw them the life preserver. You care, and so you share the Truth. We serve Jesus Christ, and therefore we always and forever will serve a purpose. We are not perfect, but we all point to The One who IS.

Listen and meditate on these verses today:

JEREMIAH 29:11 ESV
For I know the PLANS I HAVE FOR YOU, declares the Lord, plans for welfare and not for evil, to give you a future and a hope.
(He has plans for you)

PROVERBS 16:4 ESV
The Lord has made everything for its PURPOSE, even the wicked for the day of trouble.
("Everything" includes you. You were made for a purpose.)

1 PETER 2:9 ESV
But you are a chosen race, a royal priesthood, a holy nation, a people for his own possession, that YOU MAY PROCLAIM the excellencies of him who

called you out of darkness into his marvelous light.
(You should be proclaiming)
ROMANS 8:28 ESV
And we know that for THOSE WHO LOVE GOD all things work together for good, for those who are called according to his PURPOSE.
(Do you love God? Then you have a purpose!)
PSALM 138:8 ESV
The Lord will fulfill his PURPOSE FOR ME; your steadfast love, O Lord, endures forever. Do not forsake the work of your hands.
(Other believers knew what we need to know, that He will fulfill His purpose for us.)
COLOSSIANS 1:16 ESV For by him all things were created, in heaven and on earth, visible and invisible, whether thrones or dominions or rulers or authorities—ALL THINGS WERE CREATED THROUGH HIM AND FOR HIM.

(You were created for Him, not for yourself, so living for yourself will never be fulfilling your purpose.)
EPHESIANS 2:10 ESV For we are his workmanship, CREATED IN CHRIST JESUS FOR GOOD WORKS, which God prepared beforehand, that we should walk in them.
(You were created to do good works, get to it!).
1 CORINTHIANS 6:19-20 ESV Or do you not know that your body is a temple of the Holy Spirit within you, whom you have from God? You are not your own, for you were bought with a price. So GLORIFY GOD IN YOUR BODY.
(The purpose of that body is to Glorify God!!!)
ROMANS 11:36 ESV
For FROM HIM AND THROUGH HIM AND TO HIM ARE ALL THINGS. To him be glory forever. Amen.
(Direct your work and life To HIM)
MATTHEW 28:18-20 ESV
And Jesus came and said to them, "All authority in heaven and on earth has been given to me. GO THEREFORE

AND MAKE DISCIPLES of all nations, baptizing them in the name of the Father and of the Son and of the Holy Spirit, teaching them to observe all that I have commanded you. And behold, I am with you always, to the end of the age."
(Share The Gospel)
<u>1 CORINTHIANS 10:31</u> ESV
So, whether you eat or drink, or WHATEVER YOU DO, DO ALL TO THE GLORY OF GOD.

Maybe your life looks like a cloudy day at the beach. It may be time to be the sunshine in someone's cloudy day. I'm learning that rain at the beach is bearable if others you care about are with you. Go now. Realize your purpose and purpose to do it all to the glory of God!

WEEK 23

Get Over The Hump Day SINCERE Devotional:

I used to sing in church. I always got so nervous. I just had a hard time being....well, serious. Don't get me wrong. I loved it, but I hated being so nervous and honestly being so transparent in front of people. When I'm singing to God, I'm very emotional and it's heart felt. It took me a long time to realize I wasn't performing for the people sitting out in the pews. A wise old pastor (my dad) taught me the correct perspective on the church service. The pastor and the people leading in song are not the performers at all. They are facilitating and obeying God to the best of the abilities and opportunities they've been given. The audience is not the church members in the pews. The audience is God Himself. The performers are those people out in the pews or chairs or whatever you sit in at your church. God is watching us. Our hearts will perform for God and tell our story. God will see it. He will know why you came to church (or why you didn't). He will be watching, and that is important to know. We must all come ready and prepared, for we are all performing for The King whether we know it or not. That is, I believe, a much clearer and appropriate perspective to have when going to church. I believe the word I'm looking for is SINCERITY. If we would sincerely worship Jesus Christ, and sincerely care about those He cares about, then many of our arguments would fade into the background as we all began taking part in caring more about the proper order to life and less about ourselves. The proper order is constantly stated in this question, "What are your priorities?" If you ask that in church, you probably wouldn't get a soul-searching sincere answer. What you probably would hear is, "God, family, and work," because the truth is that most of us "know" certain answers. We just don't sincerely live out those answers, which makes our lives look, well.....insincere. So take a moment and reevaluate, and let's ask ourselves, "Where are my priorities?" Let's SINCERELY consider that today. Our hearts should be sincerely performing for God, so let's not waste our time. Let's see what God has shared with us about this thing called SINCERITY.

<u>2 CORINTHIANS 8:8</u>

I am not speaking this as a command, but as proving through the earnestness of others the SINCERITY OF YOUR LOVE also.
(Is your love sincere?)

EPHESIANS 6:24
Grace be with all those who LOVE OUR LORD JESUS CHRIST with incorruptible love.
(Do you sincerely love Jesus?)

JOSHUA 24:14
"Now, therefore, fear the LORD and serve Him in SINCERITY and truth; and put away the gods which your fathers served beyond the River and in Egypt, and serve the LORD.
(Do you sincerely revere The Lord and serve Him?)

1 TIMOTHY 1:5
But the goal of our instruction is love from a pure heart and a good conscience and a SINCERE FAITH.
(Is your faith sincere?)

ROMANS 12:9
Let love be without hypocrisy Abhor what is evil; cling to what is good.

(Do you sincerely hate what is evil and cling to what is good or do you compromise what is good to get along with what is evil to be more acceptable to this world?)

<u>1 PETER 1:22</u>

Since you have in obedience to the truth purified your souls for a SINCERE LOVE OF THE BRETHREN, fervently love one another from the heart,

(Do you sincerely love other Christians?)

<u>1 JOHN 3:18</u>

Little children, let us not love with word or with tongue, but in deed and truth.

(Can people see your sincerity lived out through your life's actions?)

<u>2 CORINTHIANS 1:12</u>

For our proud confidence is this: the testimony of our conscience, that in holiness and GODLY SINCERITY, not in fleshly wisdom but IN THE GRACE OF GOD, we have conducted ourselves in the world, and especially toward you.

(Do you conduct yourselves towards others sincerely?)

<u>2 CORINTHIANS 2:17</u>

For we are not like many, peddling the word of God, but as FROM SINCERITY, but as from God, WE SPEAK in Christ in the sight of God.

(Do you present things to others sincerely?)

1 THESSALONIANS 2:3-5

For our exhortation does not come from error or impurity or by way of deceit; but just as we have been approved by God to be entrusted with the gospel, so we speak, not as pleasing men, but GOD who EXAMINES OUR HEARTS. For we never came with flattering speech, as you know, nor with a pretext for greed...

(Is your heart sincere?)

This is just something to meditate on today...the fact that God sees the heart and can tell if we are sincere. The question is not, "Were you ever sincere, or have you shown to be sincere at times?" The question is, "Where is your heart right NOW? Have you grown cold, thinking the church service exists to entertain you? Do you half heartedly drudge through the songs, or even through your whole day?" Sincerely spend some time with God today, considering what He has done for you. When you consider Him, His sincerity will overtake you and consume you, and you'll know He has refreshed your heart. The beginning of sincerity always begins with getting our priorities back in line. GOD is your focus. Sincerely love and meditate on Him, and the rest will follow. May these scriptures sincerely challenge and refresh you today.

WEEK 24

Get Over The Hump Day FATHERS Devotional:

When I was about 10 years old, I was at home and it was Christmas time. One of my favorite times of the year. We had ordered a pizza, and my dad and I went to pick it up. We got in our pale blue Volkswagen bug and headed out. There were candles lit alongside the road and Christmas lights blinking, and we were listening to Christmas tunes on the radio. It took us forever because traffic was backed up, but it didn't matter because we were just hanging out. Today when I sat down to write something about fathers, that is what came to my mind. I have some great memories, but that one sticks out to me today. It's simple, and so is what I'd like to say to fathers everywhere. When Bean and Bailey do speaking and comedy at Men's Conferences, we take with us this simple message: Be There.

Yep. That's it. Be there. Be at as many games as you can. Be there to answer your kid's questions. Be there to pray with them at night and tuck them in. Be there to teach them how to throw, catch, spike, kick, or whatever else you can do with a ball. Be there to teach them how to drive. Be there to help with the homework (until it gets too hard for you.....uhm, like up until 3rd grade math I guess). Be there to encourage them. Be there to discipline them. Be there to teach them what the Scriptures say. Be there to help pick out clothes (even if it's a dress). Be there in the kitchen cooking together. Be there celebrating the win, or the graduation, or the fact that they walked or talked or swam for the first time, or finally sat through dinner without whining, or getting up, or passing gas. Do you get the point? BE THERE.

I understand that we need to work. I also am well acquainted with the fact that many of us have to travel for work. I also understand that we may have to miss a birthday or a ball game or a recital, etc. What I don't understand is the laziness of choosing to work too much. That's right, I said the laziness of working too much. Many men would prefer to work longer hours than have to put the time in training their children the correct way, or stay out just a little longer so that dinner is ready when they get home instead of getting home to make cooking the dinner fun and involving everyone. You're tired? Who cares? Let me tell you who cares. Nobody. I'm not saying you're not legitimately tired, and that occasionally you'll need to rest instead of play with the kids or help your wife do whatever she wants you to help her with. But if it's a habit, break it. There are some things men should break. Bad, lazy, and selfish habits are one of them (or is that three of them?). Either way, let's take responsibility. If you're not gonna love, cherish, and honor you're wife, then choose to be celibate. Focus on working and witnessing. If you don't think you can make time for your kids, don't make the choice to do the things that lead to having children. Because children need their father. I'm not gonna get any Dad of the Year awards anytime soon, but I'm certainly gonna try to honor God by the way I try to love my family and provide for them. Speaking of providing for them. You don't need a lot of money to do that. I'd pretty much guarantee that your wife and kids would rather have you around more than they'd rather have a new toy. I could go on all day about this, but I won't because you men understand what I'm saying already. I've struggled with my selfishness for years. I'm trying so hard to kill it. I got up this morning at 6:30am to run with my wife before she went to work (I hear you morning people thinking, “uhm that’s not that early”......but that’s a big deal for me because I’m a comedian sooo uhm, yeah I don’t generally like getting up early so give me some points here, lol). And then I came home and did my Bible study, and I’ve fed the kids breakfast and already yelled at them once, and am planning the work day here at the house. That’s not because it’s what I wanted to do today. But I know I’ll be thankful that I did it because THE WAY I FEEL DOESN’T MATTER. ITS THE WAY I FAITH THAT MATTERS. Faith comes first, then hopefully the feelings follow. If they don’t, that’s fine too because I know doing what’s right gives me a peace I can’t find anywhere else. I’m pretty sure that’s the point of the caddyshack, meshack and that billy goat in Daniel chapter 3.

Let me just leave you guys with a few Scriptures to meditate on today. Remember that God is THE FATHER and that HE IS LOVE. It’s our responsibility to not only love our wives and children and others but to understand how much our Heavenly Father loves us. Yes men, YOUR HEAVENLY FATHER LOVES YOU and He wants you to love others. So let's start there:

MARK 12:30-31

and you shall love the Lord your God with all your heart, and with all your soul, and with all your mind, and with all your strength.' The second is this, 'You shall love your neighbor as yourself.' There is no other commandment greater than these."

(Now that we have a solid foundation)

EPHESIANS 5:25,28-29

Husbands, love your wives, just as Christ also loved the church and gave Himself up for her,

28 So husbands ought also to love their own wives as their own bodies. HE WHO LOVES HIS OWN WIFE LOVES HIMSELF; 29 for no one ever hated his own flesh, but nourishes and cherishes it, just as Christ also does the church,

(Loving God comes first, then your wife, then your kids)

<u>PROVERBS 22:6</u>

Train up a child in the way he should go; even when he is old he will not depart from it.

(training = hard work)

<u>EPHESIANS 6:4</u>

Fathers, do not provoke your children to anger, but bring them up in the discipline and instruction of the Lord.

<u>DEUTERONOMY 6:7</u>

You shall teach them diligently to your children, and shall talk of them when you sit in your house, and when you walk by the way, and when you lie down, and when you rise.

(teach them God's word "diligently")

<u>COLOSSIANS 3:21</u>

Fathers, do not provoke your children, lest they become discouraged.

<u>PROVERBS 29:17</u>

Discipline your son, and he will give you rest; he will give delight to your heart.

<u>PSALM 127:3</u>

Behold, children are a heritage from the Lord, the fruit of the womb a reward.

Remember men...

<u>ROMANS 8:14</u>

For all who are led by the Spirit of God are sons of God.

You're either a son of the Living God or you're not. I pray you'll know God as your Father and then strive to be like Him. Now purpose in your hearts to BE LIKE CHRIST and to BE THERE as much as you can. Now go enjoy that new tie you're about to get for Father's Day!

WEEK 25

Get Over The Hump Day IT'S WHO YOU KNOW Devotional:

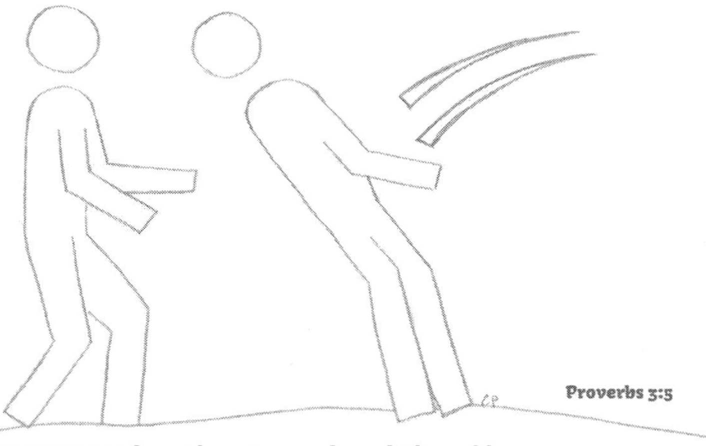

TRUST in the Lord with all your heart

Years ago I moved to Orlando to try to get a job at one of the theme parks. When I got there the guy I was supposed to move in with told me his family was going through some difficulties, and so I had to find another place to live. Thankfully another wonderful family took me in for a while. I started looking for a job and went to Universal Studios to fill out an application, and I told them I wanted to do some acting on one of the rides. They had King Kong, Jaws, etc. They told me all those positions had been filled, and I went home feeling defeated. I talked to a friend about it who had worked there before, and he gave me the name of the lady in charge of hiring actors. So I went back and filled out a second application. On this application I said I wanted to wait tables, and in small writing beside it I also put that I'd like to work on one of the rides. They finally brought me back for an interview to wait tables, and when she asked me what I wanted to do I said, "I'd like to work on one of the rides." She then responded, "Oh, well it says that you wanted to wait tables." Then I replied, "Well if you'll look there, I also put down I'd like to work on one of the rides." She then told me, as I'd heard before, that those jobs were already taken. This time I was ready, and I responded that I knew this lady (we'll call her Wanda) through one of my friends, and asked if she would go ask Wanda if I could interview for the job on one of the rides. The lady interviewing me seemed a bit agitated, but since I'd thrown out Wanda's name, and Wanda was really the one in charge, I believe she felt obligated to at least go ask her. The lady left, and came back in a few minutes telling me to come back tomorrow and interview with Wanda for one of the rides. I went back in the next day and did a reading, and Wanda gave me my choice. I chose to work on the Jaws ride, and I had a blast. The point here is that it matters WHO YOU KNOW.

It just so happens that I know someone waaaaaay more important than Wanda. I know personally and intimately The God of the Universe. Yet I still find myself in a tailspin of worry and doubt sometimes. Do you ever feel that way? I know it's crazy. I know it's even wrong. God has promised that He will take care of our needs (MATTHEW

6:25-34). He doesn't break His promises. I was taking a shower the other day, and I was thinking about God (I think the shower is one of the last places left that a person can get away from a cell phone), and I began to ask some questions to myself. Is He sufficient? Can He do all things? Does He care about me? Is He worthy to be trusted? Think about that. Is God worthy to be trusted? I think I hear you saying, "Yes!, yes HE IS!" Unfortunately it doesn't take us long to forget that, does it? And that drives me crazy. Sometimes I worry about work or my family or certain situations, as if for some reason God has fallen asleep. Good news everyone! God never sleeps (PSALM 121:4). He is indeed WORTHY to be TRUSTED, so relax and let's read some verses together.

PROVERBS 3:5 ESV

TRUST in the Lord with all your heart, and do not lean on your own understanding.

ROMANS 8:28 ESV

And we know that for those who love God all things work together for good, for those who are called according to his purpose.

PSALM 37:4-6 ESV

Delight yourself in the Lord, and he will give you the desires of your heart. Commit your way to the Lord; TRUST in him, and he will act. He will bring forth your righteousness as the light, and your justice as the noonday.

PROVERBS 3:6 ESV

In all your ways acknowledge him, and he will make straight your paths.

PSALM 46:10 ESV

"Be still, and know that I am God. I will be exalted among the nations, I will be exalted in the earth!"

HEBREWS 13:8 ESV

Jesus Christ is the same yesterday and today and forever.

MARK 5:36 ESV

But overhearing what they said, Jesus said to the ruler of the synagogue, "Do not fear, only believe."

ROMANS 15:13 ESV

May the God of hope fill you with all joy and peace in believing, so that by the power of the Holy Spirit you may abound in hope.

PSALM 9:10 ESV

And those who know your name put their TRUST in you, for you, O Lord, have not forsaken those who seek you.

PSALM 28:7 ESV

The Lord is my strength and my shield; in him my heart TRUSTS, and I am helped; my heart exults, and with my song I give thanks to him.

JEREMIAH 29:11 ESV

For I know the plans I have for you, declares the Lord, plans for welfare and not for evil, to give you a future and a hope.

PSALM 112:7 ESV

He is not afraid of bad news; his heart is firm, TRUSTING in the Lord.

HEBREWS 11:6 ESV

And without faith it is impossible to please him, for whoever would draw near to God must believe that he exists and that he rewards those who seek him.

ISAIAH 26:3 ESV
You keep him in perfect peace whose mind is stayed on you, because he TRUSTS in you.
JOSHUA 1:9 ESV
Have I not commanded you? Be strong and courageous. Do not be frightened, and do not be dismayed, for the Lord your God is with you wherever you go."
PSALM 91:1-16 ESV
He who dwells in the shelter of the Most High will abide in the shadow of the Almighty. I will say to the Lord, "My refuge and my fortress, my God, in whom I TRUST." For he will deliver you from the snare of the fowler and from the deadly pestilence. He will cover you with his pinions, and under his wings you will find refuge; his faithfulness is a shield and buckler. You will not fear the terror of the night, nor the arrow that flies by day, ...
ISAIAH 43:2-3 ESV
When you pass through the waters, I will be with you; and through the rivers, they shall not overwhelm you; when you walk through fire you shall not be burned, and

the flame shall not consume you. For I am the Lord your God, the Holy One of Israel, your Savior. I give Egypt as your ransom, Cush and Seba in exchange for you.

JOB 13:15 ESV

Though he slay me, I will hope in him; yet I will argue my ways to his face.

PSLAM 40:1-17 ESV

To the choirmaster. A Psalm of David. I waited patiently for the Lord; he inclined to me and heard my cry. He drew me up from the pit of destruction, out of the miry bog, and set my feet upon a rock, making my steps secure. He put a new song in my mouth, a song of praise to our God. Many will see and fear, and put their trust in the Lord. BLESSED IS THE MAN WHO MAKES THE LORD HIS TRUST, who does not turn to the proud, to those who go astray after a lie! You have multiplied, O Lord my God, your wondrous deeds and your thoughts toward us; none can compare with you! I will proclaim and tell of them, yet they are more than can be told. ...

JEREMIAH 17:7-8 ESV

"BLESSED IS THE MAN WHO TRUSTS IN THE LORD, WHOSE TRUST IS THE LORD. He is like a tree planted by water, that sends out its roots by the stream, and does not fear when heat comes, for its leaves remain green, and is not anxious in the year of drought, for it does not cease to bear fruit."

MARK 9:24 ESV

Immediately the father of the child cried out and said, "I believe; help my unbelief!"

Do you know Jesus Christ? If so, ask yourself, "Is He worthy of my trust?" Ask yourself that question, and keep those verses above handy anytime you begin to worry or doubt. Memorize those verses. The word is our only offensive weapon. Draw out that sword and destroy that doubt, worry, and fear with the perfect powerful promises of God. Be encouraged! He knows what's going on in your life. Have a better day as you let go of that stress and take a step closer to God by TRUSTING HIM.

WEEK 26

Get Over The Hump Day SUPREME Devotional:

When I was a kid I saw the movie Jaws. I also saw a news report about someone getting bit by a shark. Soon afterwards, as I was swimming in a friend's pool, and much like a child afraid of the dark for no reason, I found myself wanting to get out of the pool because I was in the deep end and I felt like there was a shark at the bottom just waiting to attack! Can you hear that Jaws music? Hey, it could happen! In reality, it couldn't happen. I mean, of course some James Bond enemy could show up and throw a tiny shark in the pool, etc., but in the real world that we live in there are no sharks living in chlorinated family pools. I was deceived by my own feelings and emotions into believing something that could never be true. The same thing is happening on a much larger scale to lots of people out there. We're swimming in a pool of media-driven arguments and are deceived into thinking that things around us are changing and that we should be afraid. As I sit and read opinion after opinion on media sites, I realize why I stopped watching and reading the news years ago. It's a useless flood of opinions that leads us in argumentative circles. I quit watching the news when I had children because I realized that every time I watched the news it was always bad news. It was people arguing over the way they see things, so I turned it off. (It's apparently no fun to watch when people are getting along.) I didn't read the newspapers, and I was.....happier. Then I started trying to make a difference by making people's days a little brighter on social media sites. In doing so, I was now privy once again to every news story out there, and again I find myself drawn in for some reason to read the filth of opinions that flood through my room via the computer. And so I shut it off because I found myself drawn in with the desire to give my own opinion, realizing that others have already done that and all it did was prompt someone else to give their opinion...and the roller coaster rolls on. No matter what we share, people can spin it however they want so that they can then spew out their opinion. Rest assured fellow believers. There is peace.There is good news. There is only ONE SUPREME COURT and it is not held in the USA.

No matter which way a vote goes, no matter how much people want to spin or spit out words, I will hold to the Word of God. That is The Supreme

Word, written by a Supreme Being who IS GOD and His son is Jesus Christ and He came to seek and save the lost (LUKE 19:10 For the Son of Man has come to seek and to save that which was lost.") If anything, we should be reminded that the enemy is a deceiver, and so people will be deceived.(JOHN 8:44 "...He was a murderer from the beginning, and does not stand in the truth because there is no truth in him Whenever he speaks a lie, he speaks from his own nature, for he is a liar and the father of lies.) If everyone who thought they were saved were actually saved, there would be no such thing as deception, right? Don't throw those pearls to the pigs (MATTHEW 7:6 "Do not give what is holy to the dogs; nor cast your pearls before swine, lest they trample them under their feet, and turn and tear you in pieces.) Instead remember that there is nothing new under the sun (ECCLESIASTES 1:9 That which has been is that which will be, And that which has been done is that which will be done. So there is nothing new under the sun.).

Remember that we have a job to do and it's not to change opinions on social issues. It's to change hearts by spreading the gospel (MARK 16:15 "And He said to them, 'Go into all the world and preach the gospel to every creature.'"/MATTHEW 28:19-20 "Go therefore and make disciples of all the nations, baptizing them in the name of the Father and of the Son and of the Holy Spirit, teaching them to observe all things that I have commanded you; and lo, I am with you always, even to the end of the age.") We know what the Word says, and so we understand that there is a judgment coming for everyone. (ROMANS 2:4-11 Or do you think lightly of the riches of His kindness and tolerance and patience, not knowing that the kindness of God leads you to repentance? But because of your stubbornness and unrepentant heart you are storing up wrath for yourself in the day of wrath and revelation of the righteous judgment of God, who will render to each person according to his deeds: to those who by perseverance in doing good seek for glory and honor and immortality, eternal life; but to those who are selfishly ambitious and do not obey the truth, but obey unrighteousness, wrath and indignation. There will be tribulation and distress for every soul of man who does evil, of the Jew first and also of the Greek, but glory and honor and peace to everyone who does good, to the Jew first and also to the Greek. For there is no partiality with God/ 2 CORINTHIANS 5:10 For we must all appear before the judgment seat of Christ, so that each one may be recompensed for his deeds in the body, according to what he has done, whether good or bad.) Knowing that it's coming spurs me on to share the Truth and waste less time on arguing with people who really do not care about what I believe. Be encouraged, my brothers and sisters, God hasn't changed, nor will He. His Word is clear, but the enemy is trying to make us think there are sharks in our pools, when in reality God is as clear and as majestic and as in control as He ever has been and as He ever will be. This is our warning (<u>GALATIANS 6:7</u> Be not deceived, God is not mocked; for whatsoever a man soweth, that shall he also reap.) Stay calm, believers, because HE IS. He is right. He is just. He will repay. He will save. He forgives. He sustains. He protects. He rewards. He punishes. He will destroy. He will restore. He was. He IS. He is to come. He is God. He is Supreme and HE IS ALIVE! So take heart, weary believers, and laugh out loud again today, knowing that as bad as it seems, it's not "news to Him." Persevere and remember they're going out from us because they never were with us (<u>1 JOHN 2:19</u> They went out from us, but they were not of us; for if they had been of us, they would no doubt have continued with us: but they went out, that they might be made manifest that they were not all of us..) Stand firm. Kneel humbly. Hug lovingly. Teach truthfully. Pray diligently. Do not compromise your beliefs. Do not argue. Do not hate. Have Faith. Have Hope.

Have Love. Get out from in front of that screen and get into that Bible. Pray for the lost and deceived. Many who claim to know Him, He will say to them "Depart from Me". (MATTHEW 7:21-23 Not every one that saith unto me, Lord, Lord, shall enter into the kingdom of heaven; but he that doeth the will of my Father which is in heaven. Many will say to me in that day, Lord, Lord, have we not prophesied in thy name? and in thy name have cast out devils? and in thy name done many wonderful works? And then will I profess unto them, I never knew you: depart from me, ye that work iniquity.) So check yourself to see whether you are in the faith (2 CORINTHIANS 13:5 Examine yourselves, to see whether you are in the faith. Test yourselves. Or do you not realize this about yourselves, that Jesus Christ is in you?—unless indeed you fail to meet the test!.) Then, when you're clear on that, go make a difference. Cling to what is right, and trust God to do His good will in you. (PHILIPPIANS 2:13 for it is God who is at work in you, both to will and to work for His good pleasure.)

Enjoy this day and know that God is still the only One that is Supreme.

WEEK 27

Get Over The Hump Day
A,B,C....WHERE'S D? Devotional:

I want what I want, when I want it, and how I want it. That's today's mentality, and it's also the mentality of a three year-old. When we hear a three year old say it, we laugh. But when you're still thinking that way and you're twenty-three, thirty-three, etc. something is wrong. Therefore I'm just going to say that there are many things wrong with people today. I would love to say that I don't struggle with that mentality, but that would be a lie. I do want things my way. That's why we argue, right? There are exceptions, but most of the time when we argue, it's because we have a sin problem of wanting things our way. I'm reminded of PHILIPPIANS 2:3-4 "Do nothing from selfishness or empty conceit, but with humility of mind regard one another as more important than yourselves; do not merely look out for your own personal interests, but also for the interests of others." Ouch... More on that later.....

If you have attended an evangelical event in the last 30 years, and especially if that event was Vacation Bible School, then you have heard of the ABC's of Salvation. If you haven't, it goes something like this: A - Admit to God that you are a sinner. B- Believe that Jesus is God's Son. C- Confess Jesus as your Savior and Lord. Now, put some crazy fast and fun music behind it and sing it and you have your title VBS song. I love that we share the gospel and there is no greater time than now to share, as the world needs a Savior. The good news is that the world has a Savior. The bad news is they just don't seem to want one. Let me give some reference as to where this ABC strategy comes from, and then add one more letter that we tend to leave out possibly because it messes with our desire to have things our way. We probably should start adding it in the mix so that people will better understand what's involved in following Jesus.

ROMANS 10:9-13 ...if you confess with your mouth that Jesus is Lord and believe in your heart that God raised him from the dead, you will be saved. For with the heart one believes and is justified, and with the mouth one confesses and is saved. For the Scripture says, "Everyone who believes in him will not be put to shame." For there is no distinction between Jew and Greek; for the same Lord is Lord of all, bestowing his riches on all who call on him. For "everyone who calls on the name of the Lord will be saved."

Wonderful! Do you see the word "LORD" there? HE MUST BE THE LORD OF YOUR LIFE. We also need to share this truth:

MATTHEW 16:24, MARK 8:34, and LUKE 9:23 all say DENY YOURSELF.

MATTHEW 16:24-26 Then said Jesus unto his disciples, If any man will come after me, let him deny himself, and take up his cross, and follow me.
25 For whosoever will save his life shall lose it: and whosoever will lose his life for my sake shall find it.
26 For what is a man profited, if he shall gain the whole world, and lose his own soul? or what shall a man give in exchange for his soul?

Generally, I think it's fair to let people know that living for Jesus means no longer living for yourself. Maybe this is where we've dropped the ball evangelistically. Maybe the reason we've had a lot of "decisions" but we're short helpers and volunteers, and our college students are nowhere to be found, is because we didn't mention that this salvation thing ain't over after you say a prayer. You don't just take part of the Scripture; you've got to take it all. You don't HAVE to take it. You CAN deny it and live for yourself. Most people are choosing that route (MATTHEW 7:13-14 "Enter by the narrow gate. For the gate is wide and the way is easy that leads to destruction, and those who enter by it are many. For the gate is narrow and the way is hard that leads to life, and those who find it are few.) The world will welcome you on their route. I invite you to take the narrow route. But if you do follow Jesus, understand that He will have it His way, when He wants it, and how He wants it...because HE IS GOD. So keep teaching people to confess and believe, but also at least let them know that they will also need to deny themselves if they truly are going to follow Jesus. He will not allow you on that narrow path with all your baggage and selfishness. You must deny yourself and live for Him. You must. Otherwise, as the great philosopher Fletwood Mac sang, "You can go your own way." Yes you do not have to follow Christ. Therefore just be clear that if you want to, if you feel that call, and anytime you share Him with others...don't leave out that essential part. Admit (1 JOHN 1:9), Believe (ACTS 4:12;JOHN 3:16), Confess (ROMANS 10:9-10) and Deny yourself (MATTHEW 16:24).

Too many people want Jesus on their own terms. Frankly I'm not sure why....If you want to live for yourself, why would you want Jesus too? Why do you want God teaching you and guiding you and directing your life if you truly just want to be in control of it yourself? As believers our happiness is not the goal here. Jesus gave us that example, didn't He? If happiness here on this earth...or wealth, or sex, or marriage, or a great job...was the thing to be obtained here on earth, Jesus would have done that, or had that, right? He didn't have or do any of those things. Here's why we want God telling us how to live our lives. Because He loves you.

He knows what's best for you. He knows you need to be told no at times. He knows that some pleasures will destroy you, and refraining from some pleasures will bring you real joy. However, we have to have that faith thing to do these things because our bodies and minds and the world will tell us to lead with our feelings. And that will destroy you. We give Jesus all of ourselves, or we keep it all to ourselves. It's an All-or-Nothing deal. One last thought. If you do give Him your all, He will pay for it all. If you keep it all for yourself, you must pay the bill.

A,B,C,D......yep, I like that better.

WEEK 28

Get Over The Hump Day HATERS Devotional:

Everybody out there seems to be drinking the haterade these days. Relax, brothers and sisters, that ain't no surprise. When I lived in Panama City Beach, FL I waited tables at "Sharky's."

It's a restaurant on the beach, and boy it was boomin. That's when I learned that people from Alabama don't know how to tip. Sorry, Alabamians. I'm just saying that it was pretty well known amongst the wait staff; I'm not just "hating" on Alabama. Go Vols! I digress. The point is that I was one of the two Christians working there at the time, and when I first came on board I wasn't well received. By the end of the summer I was part of the family, and I had the opportunity to share my faith both through my words and my actions. I'm not gonna act like I was a perfect example, but they knew what I believed and they loved me anyway. I don't know if any of them came to know Jesus or not. I still pray for them. When I was working in Orlando it was a different story. It was obvious that some of my co-workers hated what I stood for. They were cordial to my face, but it was obvious they hated what I believed. I pray for them too. Through the years I've seen a lot of different reactions to the fact that I'm a Christ-follower. Some people love you, some hate you, and others accept you for who you are but want nothing to do with your faith...more specifically your Friend, Savior, and Lord. Accepting people is the "in" thing to do, so it doesn't shock me when people act as if they accept me even if they don't want to hear about my beliefs. Truth is, they hate who I am. They hate who you are, believer, because they hate who Jesus IS. The world doesn't want a Lord over them. They want to be lord of their own lives, and they certainly don't think they need a Savior. At least not the One we're telling them about. Haters gonna hate. Jesus told us that a long time ago.

JOHN 15:18-25 (NASB)

"If the world hates you, you know that it has hated Me before it hated you. If you were of the world, the world would love its own; but because you are not of the world, but I chose you out of the world, because of this the world hates you. Remember the word that I said to you, 'A slave is not greater than his master.' If they persecuted Me, they will also persecute you; if they kept My word, they will keep yours also. But all these things they will do to you for My name's sake, because they do not know the One who sent Me. If I had not come and spoken to them, they would not have sin, but now they have no excuse for their sin. He who hates Me hates My Father also. If I had not done among them the works which no one else did, they would not have sin; but now they have both seen and hated Me and My Father as well. But they have done this to fulfill the word that is written in their Law, 'They hated Me without a cause.'

It is not our job to try to make the world "like" us. We're not popular. Please grow up. You didn't win state; get over it (Napoleon Dynamite reference). There's no time to be cool. Just because you're older doesn't mean you're any wiser. High school is over, and if you're in high school right now it will be over soon and they won't give you a diploma saying that you're mature. If you're not walking with Jesus, you're not any wiser. The world wants to be cool. It wants power. It wants and wants and wants. It wants to fit in, and believer, believe me...you don't and you won't fit in. Now don't get me wrong. We need to befriend the lost, and we do need to love others and share the gospel with them. But you don't win a ton of friends by telling them the truth. You win "worldly friends" by telling them what they want to hear. We want to live at peace with others, but we must also tell them the truth.

ROMANS 12:18 (NASB) If possible, so far as it depends on you, be at peace with all men.

The time for pansy Christians who just want to be liked is OVER. We need believers who can love people and tell them the Truth with a heart of compassion...who have no interest in being cool but have every interest in others coming to know Jesus... and who have a full expectation that people will hate them and reject them because that's what they did to The One that we're trying to be like. Count it all joy brothers and sisters....

JAMES 1:2-3 (ESV) Count it all joy, my brothers, when you meet trials of various kinds, for you know that the testing of your faith produces steadfastness.

We need steadfastness these days, knowing there will be haters. Stand strong, my brothers and sisters, knowing that people will hate you.

JAMES 1:12 (ESV) Blessed is the man who remains steadfast under trial, for when he has stood the test he will receive the crown of life, which God has promised to those who love him.

We don't need cool. We need steadfastness. Be steadfast. Be faithful. Be peaceful. Be bold. Be loving. Be kind. Produce the fruit of the Spirit in your life (GALATIANS 5:22-23).
Let's stop flapping our lips and go live for Christ. Enough talk. (BE YE DOERS of the word and not talkers only.....is that what it says? OK maybe not, but you get the point).

JAMES 1:22-25 (KJV) But be ye doers of the word, and not hearers only, deceiving your own selves.For if any be a hearer of the word, and not a doer, he is like unto a man beholding his natural face in a glass: For he beholdeth himself, and goeth his way, and straightway forgetteth what manner of man he was. But whoso looketh into the perfect law of liberty, and continueth therein, he being not a forgetful hearer, but a doer of the work, this man shall be blessed in his deed.

"You're welcome to come but I don't think you'll like it." "This probably isn't for you." "This is not really your kind of place." Have you heard these things said to you before? If so, great! People will say those things, and when they do, just say, "Thanks for warning me." Then leave. That place probably isn't for you, you probably won't like it, and it's not your kind of place. Be friends with the lost. Just don't try to be LIKE the lost, because, well......then you're both lost. And two lost people have a hard time finding where they're going.

Be steadfast. Don't fit in. Love those who need your Savior. Be set apart. Be hated. Be ignored. Be left out.

Just don't be like the world. The day will come when we will be glorified.

ROMANS 8:16-18 (ESV) The Spirit himself bears witness with our spirit that we are children of God, and if children, then heirs—heirs of God and fellow heirs with Christ, provided we suffer with him in order that we may also be glorified with him. For I consider that the sufferings of this present time are not worth comparing with the glory that is to be revealed to us.

PSALM 27:14 Wait patiently for the LORD. Be brave and courageous. Yes, wait patiently for the LORD.

JOSHUA 1:9 This is my command--be strong and courageous! Do not be afraid or discouraged. For the LORD your God is with you wherever you go."

PSALM 31:24 So be strong and courageous, all you who put your hope in the LORD!

Be strong. Be Courageous. Be patient. Be brave. Be glorified. Remember... haters gonna hate. That's not you. You're gonna love. You're gonna display the fruit of The Spirit, and you're gonna persevere.

WEEK 29

Get Over The Hump Day CROSSFIT Devotional:

I'm sitting here eating a snack and watching a replay of the 2014 CrossFit Games. And I'm feeling pretty lazy and out of shape. I'm kind of nodding off, because I'm getting pretty tired watching these guys exercise. I always root for Rich Froning because he's my best friend. Ok, we're not "best"

friends, but we're buddies. Ok, I'm sure we'd be buddies if he knew who I was. But I do have a connection with him. He has a gym in Tennessee where my brother works out. My brother actually really does know him, and they are friends. I've only met him once through my brother, and I totally respect what he's been able to accomplish. He's earned the title "Fittest Man on Earth" for the last 4 years! The most impressive part is that he is a Christ-follower. I do exercise, but if it wasn't for my wife pushing me to do so I'm not sure I would test myself very much. I played sports most of my young and in-shape days, but these days I mostly watch others play sports. And that seems so much easier. (And I prefer watching others make mistakes that I can crack on via social media...haha.) Honestly, I respect the effort these men and women put in to be their best. I accomplished some things in my day playing soccer, but nothing like my wife did in her sport of swimming. She won state at a young age, and has always had a drive to work hard. That kind of drive is something that does NOT come natural to me. But I think it's very worth working toward so that I can feel my best and be mentally and physically disciplined. Let me just note a few scriptures that teach us to care for our bodies.

1 CORINTHIANS 6:19-20 ESV Or do you not know that your body is a temple of the Holy Spirit within you, whom you have from God? You are not your own, for you were bought with a price. So glorify God in your body.
(Of course this is not just important physically, but that is part of it)
3 JOHN 1:2 ESV
Beloved, I pray that all may go well with you and that you may be in good health, as it goes well with your soul.
(body and soul)
1 CORINTHIANS 3:17 ESV
If anyone destroys God's temple, God will destroy him. For God's temple is holy, and you are that temple.

(Protect the temple - mentally, physically, spiritually and emotionally.)
1 CORINTHIANS 10:31 ESV So, whether you eat or drink, or whatever you do, do all to the glory of God.
(Even eating and drinking should be done to glorify God. I think we are allowed to enjoy the taste of things like Doritos, but I'm pretty sure eating a whole bag in one sitting isn't that glorifying. It's more like gluttonfying....I just now made that word up!)
PROVERBS 17:22 ESV A joyful heart is good medicine, but a crushed spirit dries up the bones.
(It's easier to be joyful when we're physically healthy)
1 CORINTHIANS 6:20 ESV For you were bought with a price. So glorify God in your body.
(This flesh thing you're wearing isn't your property, so treat it better than you would if it were yours. God will recall it one day.)

There are a couple of things I do want to point out in regards to getting healthy. The goal is not to be able to show off your body and take annoying selfies. The goal is not to use a healthy body to try and sell a product or hope people will notice you. It is quite possible that you might look great on the outside and be terribly unhealthy on the inside. The reason I exercise is that I believe it is important to try and manage well the things God bestows on us. My body is one of those things, and so I want to use it to honor Him. And I encourage you to do the same. It's free to get out and walk. Water is also free. Healthy foods are also affordable, especially with a little research. Here's the point: The better you feel, the more you'll want to be active in other things, like those things that are more important than physical exercise. Go back and read those verses. Do you notice that there seems to be something greater than the physical in each of them? "Glorifying God," "a joyful heart," and "God's temple" are all some words that should stick out to us. There are things that are important (discipling our bodies to be healthy), but there are things that are of greater importance (discipling our minds and bodies for the purpose of glorifying God). That brings this verse to mind:

1 TIMOTHY 4:8 ESV For while bodily training is of some value, godliness is of value in every way, as it holds promise for the present life and also for the life to come.

Let's spur each other on to get healthy. Spiritual health is of the most importance. As we gain more discipline I believe it will help us with other areas in our lives. That word "discipline" sure has a negative meaning to a lot of people. However, the truth is that anytime we use discipline it's almost always in an attempt to help someone better themselves. Discipline is a GOOD thing. Work has always been in God's design. Notice that Adam had a job BEFORE the fall (GENESIS 2:15). So let's get up and get with it! It's time to get up, get in that Word, and then get busy walking and talking with others to create a community of health and encouragement with other believers with the purpose of glorifying God. Let this be the day you get energized, get motivated, get moving, get to loving, get into The Word of God, and get to honoring God. You can do it. You might be into CrossFit, but are you Fit to take up your Cross and follow Him? I believe you are. You can do this!

WEEK 30

Get Over The Hump Day GRACE Devotional:

Let us then with confidence draw near to the throne of grace, that we may receive mercy and find grace to help in time of need.

HEBREWS 4:16

Christians live in a state of GRACE. We are given what we do not deserve, and that's a very good thing. I can't count how many times I've failed. Let me see if you can relate. Sometimes I struggle with a sin of some kind and find myself disobeying God on purpose because I want what I want. Then after getting "my way," I feel ashamed and defeated knowing good and well that I knew my way would not bring me true happiness. And having known the truth, I exchanged it for a lie, and I find myself depressed and broken over my sin. I repent and then turn around, and sometimes do the very same thing again...leaving me feeling like I'm useless. If you can relate, just say, "Amen, God help me" and keep reading. All sin is an offense against God, and the enemy seems to know which ones we are most susceptible to. And so we find ourselves in the midst of trouble, and life starts to get overwhelming.....until we hear God saying, "I Love You." And we feel unworthy, because indeed we are unworthy. And we cry out, "I am unworthy," and God smiles. And we cry out for forgiveness, and God says, "I forgive you." And we begin to feel broken and strengthened at the same time, understanding that God has promised to forgive us (1 JOHN 1:9 "If we confess our sins, He is faithful and just to forgive us our sins and to cleanse us from all unrighteousness.") He is eager to forgive us (PSALM 86:5 For You, Lord, are good, and ready to forgive, And abundant in lovingkindness to all who call upon You). He wants a relationship with us (1 JOHN 4:10 "In this is love, not that we loved God, but that He loved us.") He died for us WHILE WE WERE STILL SINNERS (ROMANS 5:8 but God shows his love for us in that while we were still sinners, Christ died for us.). He knows we're weak, and wants us to know He is Strong. He knows we will fall, but He will pick us up. Search out and believe His promises. They are for you. They are true. They are real. You can be useful. You will be forgiven when you ask. No, it doesn't matter how many times you fail (MATTHEW 18:21-22 Then came Peter to him, and said, Lord, how oft shall my brother sin against me, and I forgive him? till seven times? Jesus saith unto him, I say not unto thee, Until seven times: but, Until seventy times seven.)

He forgives because He is long-suffering, He is patient, He is kind. GOD IS LOVE (1 JOHN 4:7-8). It doesn't matter if you feel loved, because love isn't a feeling. Love is a Person...the very person of God. God is Spirit, and He IS the spirit of love. Rest assured, believer, you are still loved. He doesn't leave you or forsake you (DEUTERONOMY 31:6 Be strong and courageous. Do not fear or be in dread of them, for it is the Lord your God who goes with you. He will not leave you or forsake you.") There are things God can NOT do! He can Not be untrue to His nature or His promises (PSALM 89:34 My covenant I will not break, nor alter the word that has gone out of my lips.) He must be faithful, He must be true, He must forgive, and He must love. That is great news for us believers. There is, of course, another side to that for those who do not know Him. He also must punish sin for those who will not deny themselves, take up their cross and follow Him (REVELATION 20:14-15 Then death and Hades were thrown into the lake of fire This is the second death, the lake of fire. And if anyone's name was not found written in the book of life, he was thrown into the lake of fire). I'll say it again, because some of you may doubt it. God still loves you, God still wants to use you, and God still forgives you again and again and again. Grace. Accept it. Believe what God has said. Don't make the sin worse by denying the forgiveness He has promised to give you. All hail the power of Jesus' name. Grace is yours, from God. Be free from that guilt. If your boat was sinking and your child had a hold on the boat and wouldn't let go, how would you feel? Right. So let go of that guilt that is trying to drag you down, and be free again. The Bible is full of great men and women who were failures for a reason. It's so we could relate. It's so we would understand that God forgives, He picks us up, and He uses us anyway. A man after God's own heart can commit adultery and murder and be forgiven and used again for the glory of God. Read one of the most sorrowful and thoughtful prayers ever in PSALM 51. Use that as a guide when you need to pour out your heart to Him.

"Grace to you" is how Paul liked to open his letters. He knew the Scriptures better than anyone and ignored the truths in them for years. Peter knew Jesus and was ready to fight one moment, yet the next he was denying He even knew Him. Maybe that's you. It's been me before. Good news! God loves you. God forgives you. God will make you useful once again. Ask for His forgiveness, and don't forget to receive it.

Grace. It's a gift He wants you to have. So take it. Hold onto it. Never let it go. Grace be to you today, and every day. I'll leave you with this last verse: HEBREWS 4:16 - Let us then approach the throne of grace with confidence, so that we may receive mercy and find grace to help us in our time of need.

WEEK 31

Get Over The Hump Day WHO CARES Devotional:

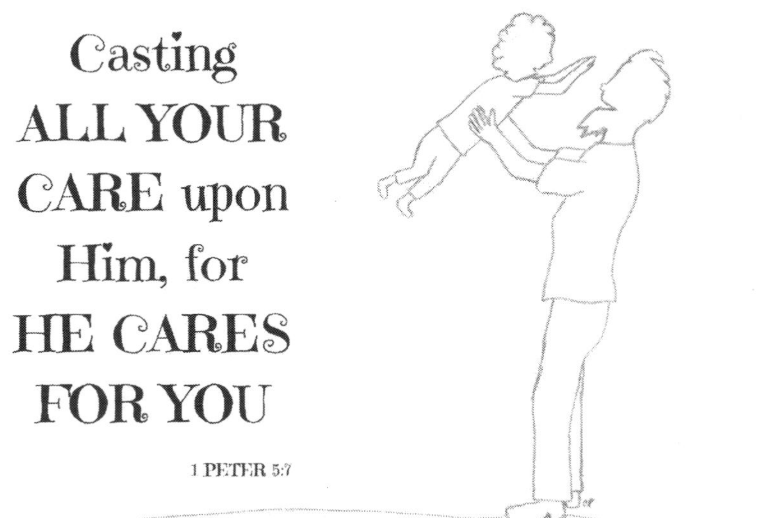

As I lay here with my knee propped up because of a volleyball injury I incurred a week ago, with my left heel bleeding from a staple sticking out of the carpet in my bedroom that I suppose was incorrectly installed by the flippers I bought this house from, I'm listening to the guys who are finally installing the fence I bought 2 months ago...all three of the guys whose ages probably total 30 years old...and I begin to laugh through the mild headache. I'm worried these guys don't know what they're doing, and concerned about my orthopedic appointment later today. And then there's throbbing still in my head and in my heel. It's this kind of day that brings this verse to mind: (1 PETER 5:6-7 Therefore humble yourselves under the mighty hand of God, that He may exalt you in due time, casting all your care upon Him, for He cares for you.)

In Sunday school one morning my grandfather gave a prayer request, but right after him another man in his class also asked for prayer. But his list went on and on about his health, the loss of his job, and his struggling marriage, etc. Just after this man shared his request, my grandfather raised his hand again and said, "Just forget about the request I just made. I think he needs your prayers more than me." That story cracks me up. It's also funny to me because my grandfather was not trying to be funny. Here's the point. We all have worries and concerns and things going on. No matter the size of the situation, God still wants to hear your prayer requests. He wants you to CAST YOUR CARES UPON HIM, BECAUSE HE CARES FOR YOU. Did you hear that? He cares about you. Sometimes I'm embarrassed to admit how much I've doubted His care. I know He cares and it seems like it should be so evident, but let me tell you, friends, deception is really, really....deceiving. These feelings and emotions we have should always be checked by THE TRUTH. Feelings can imprison you, but The Truth shall set you free (JOHN 8:31-32 So Jesus said to the Jews who had believed him, "If you abide in my word, you are truly my disciples, and you will know the truth, and the truth will set you free."). And when Jesus makes you free, you are free indeed. And I believe somewhere it says that HE IS The Truth (JOHN

14:6 Jesus said to him, "I am the way, and THE TRUTH, and the life. No one comes to the Father except through me). There it is. The answers are in the Bible if we will just look for them. Your emotions would have you sit on the couch and eat ice cream, feeling worried or sorry for yourself. But The Truth would have you work, read, and get prepared for the deception coming your way. Remember Jesus and His disciples in the garden? He told them to stay up, and watch and pray (MATTHEW 26:40-41 And he came to the disciples and found them sleeping. And he said to Peter, "So, could you not watch with me one hour? Watch and pray that you may not enter into temptation. The spirit indeed is willing, but the flesh is weak."). You are weak, but He is strong. Therefore you must walk in His ways every day to have strength. Eat Him, drink Him, and live in Him. If you don't eat, you get weak and will grab for anything, no matter how unhealthy it is. Stay hydrated in His word and eat of the fruit of The Spirit that comes forth when you commune with Him in prayer. You will find strength and reassurance that HE CARES FOR YOU. HE CARES FOR YOU. HE CARES FOR YOU. Keep saying that truth to yourself today. No matter what you've done, HE CARES FOR YOU. No matter how imperfect you are, HE CARES FOR YOU. No matter how many times you've fallen and disobeyed, HE CARES FOR YOU. I hope you get the point that HE CARES FOR YOU. I leave you with this scripture today and while you read it, be reminded how much HE CARES FOR YOU.

LUKE 15:11-32:

11 And he said, "There was a man who
had two sons. 12 And the younger of
them said to his father, 'Father, give me
the share of property that is coming to
me.' And he divided his property
between them. 13 Not many days later,
the younger son gathered all he had and
took a journey into a far country, and
there he squandered his property in
reckless living. 14 And when he had
spent everything, a severe famine arose

in that country, and he began to be in need. 15 So he went and hired himself out to one of the citizens of that country, who sent him into his fields to feed pigs. 16 And he was longing to be fed with the pods that the pigs ate, and no one gave him anything.

17 “But when he came to himself, he said, ‘How many of my father's hired servants have more than enough bread, but I perish here with hunger! 18 I will arise and go to my father, and I will say to him, “Father, I have sinned against heaven and before you. 19 I am no longer worthy to be called your son. Treat me as one of your hired servants.”’ 20 And he arose and came to his father. But while he was still a long way off, his father saw him and felt compassion, and ran and embraced him and kissed him. 21 And the son said to him, ‘Father, I have sinned against heaven and before you. I am no longer worthy to be called your son.’ 22 But the father said to his servants, ‘Bring quickly the best robe, and put it on him, and put a ring on his hand, and shoes on his

feet. 23 And bring the fattened calf and
kill it, and let us eat and celebrate.
24 For this my son was dead, and is
alive again; he was lost, and is found.'
And they began to celebrate.
25 "Now his older son was in the field,
and as he came and drew near to the
house, he heard music and dancing.
26 And he called one of the servants
and asked what these things meant.
27 And he said to him, 'Your brother has
come, and your father has killed the
fattened calf, because he has received
him back safe and sound.' 28 But he
was angry and refused to go in. His
father came out and entreated him,
29 but he answered his father, 'Look,
these many years I have served you,
and I never disobeyed your command,
yet you never gave me a young goat,
that I might celebrate with my friends.
30 But when this son of yours came,
who has devoured your property with
prostitutes, you killed the fattened calf
for him!' 31 And he said to him, 'Son,
you are always with me, and all that is
mine is yours. 32 It was fitting to

celebrate and be glad, for this your brother was dead, and is alive; he was lost, and is found.'"

WEEK 32

Get Over The Hump Day A BETTER MARRIAGE Devotional:

I'm writing this because this weekend is my 17th anniversary. Yup, 17 years. That seems like a long time, until I consider those 50-year anniversaries out there. Hopefully I can write about my 50th one day. I can't begin to write our story in a short devotional, but I can be a bit transparent and throw out some encouragement to others out there. Last year on Facebook I stated something like this: “It’s my 16th anniversary, and I want to say thanks to my wife for 14 wonderful years!” It was comical as I had people trying to correct my math, but what I said was true. Our 2nd and 3rd year of marriage were an absolute train wreck. We were not happy, and I think it’s fair to say that we both would have desired a divorce if either of us thought that was an option. We did not see that as an option because we believe the Bible and we know what it says about divorce (MALACHI 2:16 “I hate divorce, says the LORD God of Israel.”), (MARK 10:2-12 And Pharisees came up and in order to test him asked, “Is it lawful for a man to divorce his wife?” He answered them, “What did Moses command you?” They said, “Moses allowed a man to write a certificate of divorce and to send her away.” And Jesus said to them, “Because of your hardness of heart he wrote you this commandment. But from the beginning of creation, 'God made them male and female.' 'Therefore a man shall leave his father and mother and hold fast to his wife, and the two shall become one flesh.' So they are no longer two but one flesh. What therefore God has joined together, let not man separate." And in the house the disciples asked him again about this matter. And he said to them, "Whoever divorces his wife and marries another commits adultery against her, and if she divorces her husband and marries another, she commits adultery.") Also see GENESIS 2, MATTHEW 19, LUKE 16, EPHESIANS 5 and on and on it goes. Now, this is not a discussion on divorce and when it is or is not "ok" to divorce. The point is that in our case there was no reason on either side for divorce. We were both just selfish and stubborn people unwilling to trust God's promises. And we continued to be led by our emotions...a choice that will doom any marriage. A very long story short, we each turned individually to Christ, realizing that if we were going to

choose to honor and serve Christ that meant we had to honor and serve each other because Christ lives in our hearts. I have to serve the Christ that lives in her, and she in turn, has to serve the Christ that lives in me...whether we "feel" like serving each other or not. In doing this, we both began to move towards Christ, which eventually led us back together. (GENESIS 2:22 And the rib that the Lord God had taken from the man he made into a woman and brought her to the man. Then the man said,
"This at last is bone of my bones
and flesh of my flesh;
she shall be called Woman,
because she was taken out of Man."
Therefore a man shall leave his father and his mother and hold fast to his wife, and they shall become one flesh.)

Together we are one. That's not true with someone you're just living with, or dating, etc. If you're not willing to commit, then you're not willing to serve anyone but yourself...period. Just like a real commitment to Christ means you must die to yourself (1 CORINTHIANS

15:31, ROMANS 6:11-14), a true commitment to your marriage means you must die to your selfishness. This thing isn't about how you feel. Although God cares about your feelings, your feelings do not matter. Get it? What I mean is that the way you feel will never change The Truth. Therefore your feelings do not matter. However God does care about how you feel and He loves you, but He does not condone making decisions based on how happy you think something will make you or how unhappy you are in your marriage. He bases things on something SOLID. THE TRUTH WILL SET YOU FREE (JOHN 8:32). It will set you free from your own selfish desires. It will set you free from having to have things your own way (cause life ain't a Burger King slogan). It will set you free from believing stupid things like a book titled, "Your Best Life Now", because that's only true if you don't know Jesus. Your best life is not and never will be here and now. Your best life is what we believers are all looking forward to, and why we make the decisions we make while we're living this life here. Your best life will be the next one, but if you want to make this time here as "life-filled" as possible, then base your decisions in all areas of your life on THE TRUTH that will set you free, and not on your feelings...which will certainly deceive you and leave you bitter and unfulfilled. I hope and pray you make your decisions based on God's truth, and that the feelings and emotions that you desire will follow. My wife and I are truly happily married, until one of us does something stupid! Then we're still married and we have to humble ourselves against the advice of our emotions to regain that happiness. But praise be to Jesus Christ and God our Father that He has truly blessed our efforts to be faithful to His Truth. We truly love Him and each other. I pray for your marriages out there and encourage you to press on towards honoring God in your decisions. May He bless you, as you obey Him.

WEEK 33

Get Over The Hump Day WHY IT'S WEIRD TO SAY, "I'M IN LOVE WITH JESUS" Devotional:

Why it feels weird to say, "I'm in love with Jesus."

I was working with Bean one day, and we had taken a break to go and get some lunch. There's a great little Asian restaurant where we like to eat when we work in Morristown, TN. We ran into a friend that particular day and got into a conversation about Christ and His church. We began to talk about Christ being the groom and the church as His bride, and our friend said, “That’s just weird to me.” Later that day I sat down to ponder why that was strange. The truth is that our friend had a point. It is weird to think of being the “BRIDE” of Christ. Furthermore, as a man, it can be awkward to say things like, “I’m in love with Jesus,” or anything that has intimate vocabulary attached to it when thinking of another man...even if that man is Jesus. The fact is that our enemy has done a good job in veiling what LOVE really is by diverting our attention to the physical and emotional things of this world instead of focusing on the spiritual reality of the true meaning of things. This became clearer to me when I read this passage of scripture one day.

<u>2 CORINTHIANS 5:11-21</u>

11 Therefore, knowing the fear of the
Lord, we persuade others. But what we
are is known to God, and I hope it is
known also to your conscience. 12 We

are not commending ourselves to you again but giving you cause to boast about us, so that you may be able to answer those who boast about outward appearance and not about what is in the heart. 13 For if we are beside ourselves, it is for God; if we are in our right mind, it is for you. 14 For the love of Christ controls us, because we have concluded this: that one has died for all, therefore all have died; 15 and he died for all, that those who live might no longer live for themselves but for him who for their sake died and was raised. 16 FROM NOW ON, THEREFORE, WE REGARD NO ONE ACCORDING TO THE FLESH. Even though we once regarded Christ according to the flesh, we regard him thus no longer.
17 Therefore, if anyone is in Christ, he is a new creation. The old has passed away; behold, the new has come. 18 All this is from God, who through Christ reconciled us to himself and gave us the ministry of reconciliation; 19 that is, in Christ God was reconciling the world to himself, not counting their trespasses

against them, and entrusting to us the message of reconciliation. 20 Therefore, we are ambassadors for Christ, God making his appeal through us. We implore you on behalf of Christ, be reconciled to God. 21 For our sake he made him to be sin who knew no sin, so that in him we might become the righteousness of God.

I'd like to point out verse 16 and also say that since this is a short devotional, we won't delve into everything in that incredible passage of scripture. But I'd like to highlight verse 16 again, which says, " FROM NOW ON, THEREFORE, WE REGARD NO ONE ACCORDING TO THE FLESH..." I'd like to say that one reason it seems strange to assign affectionate terms to Jesus Christ is because we are still viewing Him as a man and we are still misunderstanding what true love really is. There is a pure love that flows from the heart of God. There is a purer understanding that has nothing at all to do with any kind of sexual assignment or physicality. Remember 1 JOHN 4:8

teaches us that GOD IS LOVE, and JOHN 4:24 teaches us that GOD IS SPIRIT. Therefore, true love cannot always be seen or touched. We have misinterpreted real love and assigned physical thoughts and attributes to it...thanks to our sinful fleshly minds. Love is much purer and much more than any physical relationship. God's love transcends things like sex and physical desire. The love we will have for each other in our perfected spiritual state will be more gratifying spiritually than any physical experience that you could ever have here on this earth. I think of the love relationship between Jesus and His Father. Christ never wanted to be separated from His father because there was a love relationship between them that went well beyond what our human minds can fathom (the main reason why he wanted "this cup to pass" from Him LUKE 22:42). He did not want to be separated from that love, not even for a moment. However, because of His great love towards us, He subjected Himself to the greatest pain of all time, which is separation from God. Our love towards friends and family and people in general can be so much more if we will begin seeing from a spiritual perspective, which can only be achieved if you know and are known by Jesus Christ. In Him there is a better understanding of true love. Therefore, when a man says, "I'm in love with Jesus," it can be less "weird" if we better understand the purity of what is really being stated. Purity. Love. Have you ever seen a husband take care of his sick and ailing wife? Have you ever seen a son or daughter care for their terminally ill parents? Love is about the purity of sacrifice and choosing each day to love again no matter how you feel. I know we're just touching the surface of this subject, but I hope we can use it to motivate ourselves to think about love in a clearer, more purer manner.

Maybe it's time to ask yourself that question. Are you in love with Jesus Christ? It's a question we should all ask ourselves. One thing I can tell you. He is in love with you.

<u>WEEK 34</u>

Get Over The Hump Day BUCKET LIST Devotional:

What's on your BUCKET LIST?

When I was in high school I was worried I'd die or Jesus would come back before I had a chance to do certain things here on earth that I didn't want to miss. Frankly, getting married was one of those things...because of what you were allowed to do Scripturally after you were married. I'm just being honest here. Don't judge the high school me! I don't think I'm alone in that thought process, though. The movie "The Bucket List" and the song "Live Like You Were Dyin" give us insight into my high school thought pattern. Of course most of these thoughts are absolutely ridiculous. I believe my high school thoughts were normal, but crass and so far off what is really fulfilling. "The Bucket List" and "Live Like You Were Dyin" are both entertaining and both actually attempt to make good points. For instance in that song he actually says, "I finally read the good book," and things about being a better dad, etc. But the emphasis seems to be that "reading the good book" was an afterthought, whereas the real exciting thing is that he went...."Sky divin, I went rocky mountain climbin"......blah blah blah. Now I'm not saying don't watch that movie or listen to that song. What I'm saying is that I grew out of my ignorant state by studying Scripture. My thoughts on what was exciting or important were frivolous, immature, and ignorant, and I didn't "grow" out of that mentality because I got older. Take a look around. Older doesn't necessarily mean wiser. Sometimes it just means.....you got older. I grew because God is alive in me. I grew because I devoured the Words of God. That's right, I "finally read the good book." However, I didn't just read the words. I listened to the voice behind the words, because I knew the God-man speaking them. I came to the realization that I knew The God who created the universe. I could speak to the One who created that mountain you wanna climb and that air you fall through while you're sky divin. He's The One that teaches us how to love deeper and speak sweeter. Without the power of His Spirit you can try to do those things but will never be real or consistent. You can attempt to "modify behavior" (I do have a degree in psychology, so I can throw out those phrases!), but there will never be a problem that is clearly healed or overcome for good. Why? Because they stem from sin! Sin can't be fixed by modifying behavior. It can only be fixed by the healing of a Savior! Now, this is not a study on psychology or psychiatry. My point is simply that our minds are warped by sin and can only be fixed by The One who forgives sin so that we can therefore truly live an exhilarating life. Chasing after excitement will never fulfill you or be the answer. Have you ever been asked the question, "What would you do if you found out you had only 24 hours to live?" I kind of think we should be living in a way that would prompt us to answer, "The same thing I do every day!" Does that sound boring? I'm sure there are a few things that we'd do differently. There are things one would want to get in order, etc., but I certainly wouldn't waste my time "sky divin" or "rocky mountain climbin." PHILIPPIANS 1:21 teaches us that "to live is Christ but to die is GAIN." So the excitement and exuberance will come AFTER we die, not before. One look at our Savior will provide more adrenaline and excitement than any amount of time climbing a mountain or falling from any plane...or anything else you could dream up here on this earth. Living for Him here is exciting! I recently read a great answer to the question, "Is the Christian life boring?"

Here is a quote from "Gotquestions.org":

"Those who believe the Christian life is boring have never taken God's invitation to "taste and see that the LORD is good" (PSALM 34:8). Instead, they selfishly pursue whatever they think will make them "not bored" or happy or content. The problem is, the things of this world are temporary and can never truly satisfy. The Bible tells us that sowing to please our sinful nature will surely lead to destruction (GALATIANS 6:8). King Solomon, the wisest and richest person who ever lived, had everything a person could possibly want. He said, "I denied myself nothing my eyes desired; I refused my heart no pleasure" (ECCLESIASTES 2:10). Solomon had it all, but he concluded that it was "meaningless" and likened it to "chasing after the wind" (v. 11). In other words, he had everything this world had to offer, and he was bored."

Sometimes a new Christian is surprised that his new life is not "more exciting," as if the Christian life is supposed to be a thrill-a-minute extravaganza. No life is that. Boredom is something we must all overcome. Everyone stands in line at the grocery store, gets caught in traffic, or is given jobs he'd rather not do.

Some people assume that being a Christian is boring because they've heard that Christians have to give up all the "fun" things in life. It's true that Christians give up some things, but it's not the fun that we give up. Christians give up their sin, their self-destructive behavior, their addictions, their negative attitudes, and their ignorance of God. In return, they receive "righteousness, peace and joy in the Holy Spirit" (ROMANS 14:17). They "live as children of light" in a dark world (EPHESIANS 5:8). The mistakes of their past no longer have a stronghold in their lives. They no longer live for themselves but for the One who died for them. They serve others and make a difference (ROMANS 14:7; PHILIPPIANS 2:4). They are becoming everything that God created them to be.....

The only thing in this world that has eternal value is a relationship with Jesus Christ. A growing, committed Christian will find that life is never boring. There's always another step of faith to take, another relationship to build, another person to serve." (Excerpt taken from www.gotquestions.org 2002-2015)."

I couldn't have said it better myself. Make this day count, and turn that bucket list into your daily activities list...storing up rewards for yourself in heaven, "where neither moth nor rust destroys and where thieves do not break in and steal. FOR WHERE YOUR TREASURE IS, THERE YOUR HEART WILL BE ALSO." MATTHEW 6:20-21

WEEK 35

Get Over The Hump Day PG-13 Devotional:

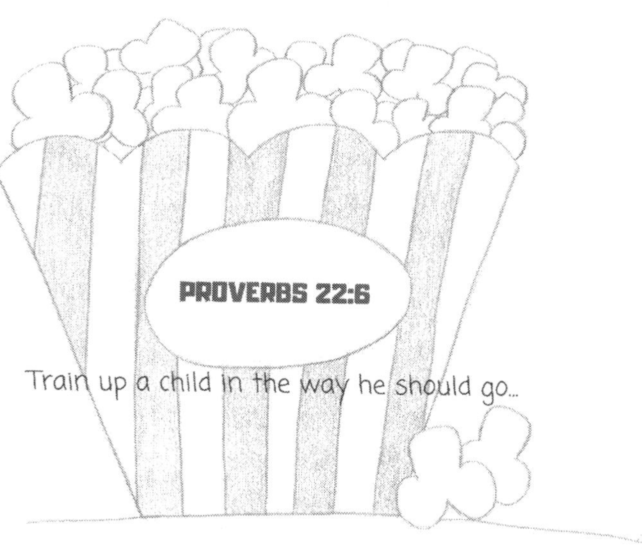

So I'm in this PG-13 movie the other day, and there is a lady with her son to my immediate left and a family with 3 children to my right. Every one of these children were under the age of 7. I won't say what movie I was watching, but I will say that it had dinosaurs in it. It wasn't long before a couple of the children were crying, and I finally found a different seat so I could enjoy the movie without passing constant judgement on parents who had decided to take the day off and traumatize their children. "Come on kids, let's watch dinosaurs eating people. It'll be fun!!" I just want to know how long we will, as parents, sacrifice our children to the god of entertainment. Frankly, if the non-Christian "Motion Picture Association of America" has rated a movie PG-13, why on earth would we, as Christian parents, think it would be ok to bring kids under 13 to a PG-13 movie? I just don't get it. We're supposed to be setting the example for our kids, aren't we? So what we're saying is that as long as it's supposed to be really entertaining, then it's ok to watch? Moms and Dads take their kids to watch boy bands or Taylor Swift in concert and yell and scream, and then sit in front of me and say things like: "I just don't understand why my daughter is so boy crazy." Well, uhm because you've been teaching her to be boy crazy with every concert and movie you take her to, and now you want to tell her it's wrong. I don't think that's gonna work, do you? Something about actions and words comes to mind. Being set apart is something we're supposed to be, isn't it? Do not be conformed to this world...

(ROMANS 12:2 ESV Do not be conformed to this world, but be transformed by the renewal of your mind, that by testing YOU MAY DISCERN what is the will of God, what is good and acceptable and perfect.)

Has that changed? I don't think so. Have you read the lyrics to the songs your kids are listening to? Taylor Swift has 2 recent top 10 songs that basically say "I've got a long list of ex-lovers," and it's ok that we've both been with different people cause you look so cool and I fall for that over and over again. So while some songs are cute and fun, others are teaching that having casual sex is ok and being cool is really what's important, etc. I think we as parents are losing that thing called "discernment." Now don't get me wrong. I love movies and TV and music, and I'm not here to criticize people who take their kids to movies or watch tv or listen to music. But when you're letting your seven year old watch CSI, you're lacking in the parenting department. It's a show about "Crime Scenes." I bring up that example because I know someone who has done that on a regular basis. Can we PLEASE think about what's good for our kids over what's convenient and fun for us? Can we? Let's think before we act. Don't expose your kids to things that you don't have to at early ages. Protect them. Change your lifestyle and what you watch until they get older. Then, watch it with them and use it as a teaching tool if you're going to watch it. Encourage others to do the same, and be ready when you do, to get that look like, "He's crazy." Yes, even church friends will give you crazy looks. If we aren't to live for this world (1 JOHN 2:15-17 (KJV) Love not the world, neither the things that are in the world. If any man love the world, the love of the Father is not in him. For all that is in the world, the lust of the flesh, and the lust of the eyes, and the pride of life, is not of the Father, but is of the world. And the world passeth away, and the lust thereof: but he that doeth the will of God abideth for ever.), then what are we doing at PG-13 and R rated movies with our small children? If you're reading this: PLEASE STOP EXPOSING YOUR KIDS BEFORE THEY'RE READY. By the way, if your child is under the age of 13 and has an Instagram account or FB account, etc. I'm pretty sure they had to lie about their age to create it. I'm just saying... If that's ok with you now, will that be ok with you when they do that later in life?

Let's play appropriate video games, play board games, go outside and play sports, or just...play. Climb a tree, watch a G or PG movie, go swimming, eat out, go to a theme park, eat ice cream, sing together, build something, read a book, act out a Bible story. But for heaven's sake stop the madness and don't be in such a hurry to expose your kids to entertainment that even the world says they're not ready for.....Your children will become like you, so spend time becoming the person you'd like your children to be. Because our kids will not value what we tell them to value; they will value what they see us value. This isn't just about movies and tv. It's about "training" a child in the way they should go (PROVERBS 22:6 (KJV) Train up a child in the way he should go: and when he is old, he will not depart from it.) Last I checked, training for something was pretty hard work. Christians, talk with your kids about The Bible all the time (DEUTERONOMY 6:6-9 (NIV) These commandments that I give you today are to be on your hearts. Impress them on your children. Talk about them when you sit at home and when you walk along the road, when you lie down and when you get up. Tie them as symbols on your hands and bind them on your foreheads. Write them on the door frames of your houses and on your gates.) Show them what patience is like by doing things at the appropriate time and age the best that you can. Stay strong. Don't give in too early. Grow together in The Lord.

This is intended to be a motivational moment for us to beware of what we're doing with our kids, not some rant against the arts. I am indeed not perfect in these areas but if we work hard, stay patient, and desire to honor God together as Christian parents and challenge each other, I believe our kids will be better for it. I'm beginning to think that most parents would rather their kids just "fit in" instead of be "set apart." Let's change things together. Here's to hoping you have a rated "G" kind of day.

WEEK 36

Get Over The Hump Day
ARGUMENTATIVE Devotional:

I used to love to argue. I even prepared at a younger age to become a lawyer because I thought I was so good at presenting an argument. The truth is I just wanted to win. It happens all the time. People yell their viewpoints at other people, convinced they are right, and not caring about the other person or what they are saying. Their only concern is to "win" the argument and to be "right." And nothing could be more....wrong. We, as Christians, seem to be taking this approach too many times. When we share the gospel, when we confront sin, and when we talk about social issues. I always remember my dad telling me, "Son, whatever you can talk somebody into, someone else can talk them out of....." and that is so true. The gospel is SHARED by believers, not argued. God calls (JUDE 1:1, ROMANS 1:6, ROMANS 8:30, EPHESIANS 4:1, etc), God draws (JOHN 6:44), and we get to take part in it by sharing the truth (MARK 16:15). We loooove to be right, though, don't we? Never mind the fact that we're not even the ones who are right. God is right. God is true. We are just sharing truth, and you can't force someone else to hear it, know it, want it, or love it. We are not "right." We are obedient to share what God has established as "right." HE IS right. We could save a lot of time by praying for wisdom (JAMES 1:5). Then we could trust in God's plan and just share the truth, understand that people will insult us (MATTHEW 5:11), and love them anyway. Pray for them (JAMES 5:16). I don't mind telling you that lying, stealing, adultery, homosexuality, drunkenness, etc. is wrong, because it's clear in The Bible. However, if you really don't believe me, then I should pray for you. Arguing over something that's clear muddies the waters and makes things....well....unclear. Truth can only be stated. 2 + 2 = 4. Do you want to argue about that? Feel free to do so, but I'm out. I can't keep telling you the same thing over and over and over, because if you refuse to see it or believe it, I don't have the power to make you see. But I can petition The One who does.

Didn't the religious leaders see the miracles of Jesus? Didn't they know He opened the eyes of the blind (JOHN 9)? They knew He raised Lazarus (JOHN 11). They didn't want to believe. They were comfortable in their sin and in their lives. They wouldn't give up their power for any convincing argument. I'm thinking bringing the dead back to life would convince them, but IT DIDN'T! That's not something I can explain. I can say this, though: "Save your money on those antacids and let your trust in The One who is in control take over your mind and your mouth".

<u>2 TIMOTHY 2:14-19; 22-26</u>

14 Remind them of these things,
and charge them before God NOT TO
QUARREL about words, which DOES
NO GOOD, but only ruins the hearers.
15 Do your best to present yourself to
God as one approved, a worker who
has no need to be ashamed, rightly
handling the word of truth. 16 But
AVOID IRREVERENT BABBLE, for it
will lead people into more and more
ungodliness, 17 and their talk will
spread like gangrene. Among them are
Hymenaeus and Philetus, 18 who have
swerved from the truth, saying that the
resurrection has already happened.
They are upsetting the faith of some.
19 But GOD'S FIRM FOUNDATION

STANDS, bearing this seal: "The Lord knows those who are his," and, "Let everyone who names the name of the Lord depart from iniquity."

22 So flee youthful passions and PURSUE RIGHTEOUSNESS, FAITH, LOVE, AND PEACE, along with those who call on the Lord from a pure heart.
23 HAVE NOTHING TO DO WITH FOOLISH, IGNORANT CONTROVERSIES; YOU KNOW THAT THEY BREED QUARRELS. 24 And the Lord's servant must NOT BE QUARRELSOME, but kind to everyone, able to teach, patiently enduring evil,
25 correcting his opponents with gentleness. God may perhaps grant them repentance leading to a knowledge of the truth, 26 and they may come to their senses and escape from the snare of the devil, after being captured by him to do his will.

Let's stand for The One that is right. Let's also remember that standing does not involve arguing. A man can stand without saying a word. There may be a place for debates, but our everyday life is not that place. Let's share His Truth and trust Him to do the convincing. Let's use our words gently and honorably. Yes, we need to be honest... but not rude. We don't need to win an argument or be seen as the one who is right. What we "need" to do is share the Good News and let the prayer of the righteous do much good. Let's go forth and make disciples, and let me remind you that the greatest stand you can take begins with a kneeling posture. May God bless you today!

WEEK 37

Get Over The Hump Day LET FORGIVENESS WIN Devotional:

I heard another story today of another Christian who had faltered. Just last week I talked with another friend in the ministry who is struggling because he was fired for reasons we won't be discussing today. I spent the normal hours writing today's devotional, and I was ready to go with it. But then I felt like God was guiding me to scrap it for now and just post one chapter of His perfect word that I hope many people will read today. I pray that as you read you will make this prayer from your own heart and accept the forgiveness that God WILL give...if you just ask Him.

I used to be confused as to why David, a man with an unhealthy desire for women and a failure in many ways as a father, was always called, "A man after God's own heart." If I'm being honest, I had a real hard time with that but couldn't deny it because it says it right there in ACTS 13:22. But even with all his faults we could point to many characteristics of David that probably could provide good enough proof that he was indeed that kind of man. But the one that I believe really shows that he was a man after God's own heart is how he responded to being called out on his sin against God. His response is recorded for us in PSALM 51. If you're struggling today to allow yourself to be forgiven, please take some time right now because I assure you that nothing else is as important as this is at this moment. Repent and be forgiven and allow God's forgiveness to wash over you right now.

PSALM 51 (ESV)

(To the choirmaster. A Psalm of David, when Nathan the prophet went to him, after he had gone in to Bathsheba.)

1
Have mercy on me, O God,
according to your steadfast love;
according to your abundant mercy
blot out my transgressions.
2
Wash me thoroughly from my iniquity,
and cleanse me from my sin!
3
For I know my transgressions,
and my sin is ever before me.
4
Against you, you only, have I sinned
and done what is evil in your sight,
so that you may be justified in your words
and blameless in your judgment.
5
Behold, I was brought forth in iniquity,

and in sin did my mother conceive me.
6
Behold, you delight in truth in the inward being,
and you teach me wisdom in the secret heart.
7
Purge me with hyssop, and I shall be clean;
wash me, and I shall be whiter than snow.
8
Let me hear joy and gladness;
let the bones that you have broken rejoice.
9
Hide your face from my sins,
and blot out all my iniquities.
10
Create in me a clean heart, O God,
and renew a right spirit within me.
11
Cast me not away from your presence,
and take not your Holy Spirit from me.
12
Restore to me the joy of your salvation,

and uphold me with a willing spirit.
13
Then I will teach transgressors your ways,
and sinners will return to you.
14
Deliver me from bloodguiltiness, O God,
O God of my salvation,
and my tongue will sing aloud of your righteousness.
15
O Lord, open my lips,
and my mouth will declare your praise.
16
For you will not delight in sacrifice, or I would give it;
you will not be pleased with a burnt offering.
17
The sacrifices of God are a broken spirit;
a broken and contrite heart, O God, you will not despise.
18
Do good to Zion in your good pleasure;
build up the walls of Jerusalem;

19
then will you delight in right sacrifices,
in burnt offerings and whole burnt
offerings;
then bulls will be offered on your altar.

Be forgiven and extend your forgiveness to others today!

WEEK 38

Get Over The Hump Day THE WAY TO #LAUGHMORE Devotional:

Thank You God for Your Word! As I move forward I will continue to use the heart I have for Jesus Christ and the crazy mind that He's given me to glorify Him and make others laugh and think. There is a method in the madness, as they say. I have tried to share always with a desire to move others towards the Scriptures, which is where I believe the answers are to life. THE BIBLE IS OF UTMOST IMPORTANCE:

2 TIMOTHY 3:16–17 All Scripture is inspired by God and profitable for teaching, for reproof, for correction, for training in righteousness; so that the man of God may be adequate, equipped for every good work.

PROVERBS 30:5–6 Every word of God is tested; He is a shield to those who take refuge in Him. Do not add to His words Or He will reprove you, and you will be proved a liar.

PSALM 19:7 The law of the Lord is perfect, restoring the soul; The testimony of the Lord is sure, making wise the simple.

THE BIBLE OFFERS US ANSWERS FOR ETERNAL LIFE (ROMANS 10:9; JOHN 3:16).

This is, after all, why we are here. Since there is an eternal life, it only makes sense that we use this temporary one to help others understand about the next one, right? Talk about making a difference! Telling one person about the next life makes a much bigger difference than ......well, anything else we could ever do! So I'd like to share what Bean and Bailey (My day job) like to talk about every time we get a chance from the stage. LAUGHTER IS A GIFT FROM GOD. What a wonderful gift. Thanks, God, for laughter! It does so many things for us physically, mentally, emotionally, and even spiritually. However, we have to keep creating laughter, because laughter only lasts a moment. Therefore when we perform we want people to know about God's gift of laughter, but most importantly we want people to know about God's greatest gift. JESUS CHRIST IS THE GREATEST GIFT FROM GOD. The Bible teaches us that we can be saved from our sins through Jesus Christ.

JOHN 3:16 (ESV) "For God so loved the world, that he gave his only Son, that whoever believes in him should not perish but have eternal life.

If we will confess Jesus as Lord, we can receive the greatest gift of all time.

ROMANS 10:9 (KJV) That if thou shalt confess with thy mouth the Lord Jesus, and shalt believe in thine heart that God hath raised him from the dead, thou shalt be saved.

This gift produces a river of life that will constantly flow in you

JOHN 4:13-14 Jesus said to her, “Everyone who drinks of this water will be thirsty again, but whoever drinks of the water that I will give him will never be thirsty again. The water that I will give him will become in him a spring of water welling up to eternal life.”

Joy for all eternity can be yours, and we want so desperately for you to know Him and to be known by Him. There’s nothing greater than to be known and loved by God Himself. There is no formula or magical prayer. Just let your heart cry out to Him and ask for His forgiveness. Confess with your mouth and believe in your heart.

He wants to save you

1 TIMOTHY 2:3–4 This is good and acceptable in the sight of God our Savior, who desires all men to be saved and to come to the knowledge of the truth.

He will cleanse you

1 JOHN 1:9 If we confess our sins, he is faithful and just to forgive us our sins and to cleanse us from all unrighteousness.

He will help you renew your mind

ROMANS 12:2 Do not be conformed to this world, but be transformed by the renewal of your mind, that by testing you may discern what is the will of God, what is good and acceptable and perfect.

He will bring you home and you will live forever with Him.

As a comedian I look for things that are funny. It's funny to me that Jesus Christ has given us His word, plenty of proof, and an opportunity to have life more abundantly (JOHN 10:10)...and the majority of people will turn away from that to pursue a short-lived and disappointing life. And that's

the kind of funny that's not really funny at all, and produces tears instead of chuckles. I challenge you today to find a reason to smile again. You can find that in Jesus Christ. Then I believe you'll find yourself laughing a lot more often.
Share this with someone today and #laughmore

WEEK 39

Get Over The Hump Day "THE LORD IS MY SHEPHERD I SHALL NOT WANT" Devotional:

PSALM 23

HE WILL RESTORE YOUR SOUL

When I was a kid I read the verse: "The Lord is my shepherd, I shall not want...." and I stopped reading. I was confused. This Lord we're talking about here, I thought...If He's so great and awesome and in fact, God...then why don't I want Him? Why doesn't

David want Him? He's the shepherd we don't want? This is a true story, people. I hate to admit my mental issues, but I've had them my whole life so I doubt they're much of a secret anymore. That's kind of funny now. But in my mind there was real confusion over that...just because I read it incorrectly. So I give you 3 thoughts to take with you today.

1. Reading and Studying the Bible correctly is extremely important. Misreading a verse can make you wonder why we shouldn't want God in our lives. Hey, it happened to me! Study diligently The Word.
2. The fact is that most people don't want God in their lives. We live in a day where people don't want to be interrupted, and certainly don't want to give anyone else control of their lives. Because they don't understand that we will all be a slave to something or someone, but when you're a slave to Christ you find that you're actually free. (JOHN 8:36 So if the Son sets you free, you will be free indeed.) Go tell others this truth.

WARNING: Many of them won't listen to you, but the ones that do will never be the same.

3. If you know Christ, you shall not want. He is with you today, just like He was yesterday and all the days before. Be encouraged, for He will make you lie down in green pastures and lead you beside the still waters. He will restore your soul. Go to Him in prayer, thank Him for who HE IS, and let your soul be restored. Be assured; you do want Him, and for some crazy reason, He wants us too! Now, there IS something funny about that.....

PSALM 23 (ESV)

A Psalm of David.

The Lord is my shepherd; I shall not
want (for anything)-added here by me.
2
He makes me lie down in green
pastures.
He leads me beside still waters.
3

He restores my soul.
He leads me in paths of righteousness
for his name's sake.
4
Even though I walk through the valley of
the shadow of death,
I will fear no evil,
for you are with me;
your rod and your staff,
they comfort me.
5
You prepare a table before me
in the presence of my enemies;
you anoint my head with oil;
my cup overflows.
6
Surely goodness and mercy shall follow
me
all the days of my life,
and I shall dwell in the house of the Lord
forever.

WEEK 40

Get Over The Hump Day YOU'VE GOT IT ALL Devotional:

We were performing at a large youth conference in Gatlinburg, TN. It was a great time and we were enjoying talking to some of the students afterwards when this boy in middle school walked up to me and said, "Man, you've got it all!" After waiting there a moment and processing what he said, I looked back at him and said, "Dude, that's the dumbest thing I've ever heard." OK, I'm totally KIDDING. I didn't say that, however to be honest that is kind of what I was thinking. I actually just said, "Thanks" and went to eat. As I was eating, what he said began to bother me. He had just seen me perform in front of a bunch of people and have a great time, but he didn't really know anything about me. I'm afraid that we look at people who are seemingly having fun, or are popular, or have money, and just think that they "have it all." I'm not sure why we're so easily deceived that way. The evidence to the contrary is overwhelming! How many Hollywood stars have to overdose, get a divorce, get DUI's, and get arrested for us to ever wake up and realize that those people, or any of us for that matter, who are living for ourselves DO NOT "have it all." That kid was right about one thing. I do have it all. I have Jesus Christ. I could stop performing tomorrow and be just as happy as ever because as long as I have Him...I have it all. And so do you. I pray if you don't know Jesus that you would begin reading His word today and find out more about how you can have it all. For my fellow believers out there, be encouraged today, understanding that if you know Jesus Christ you truly have all that you'll ever need! We just simply don't need anything else to thrive in this life, because He gives life and He gives it more abundantly (JOHN 10:10). So if you're feeling down today, just remember that "You've Got It All." (I don't know who that kid is, but if i could go back in time to that moment I'd look him in the eye, take the time, and make sure he understood that he could have it all too.)

1 CORINTHIANS 8:6
yet for us there is one God, the Father.
All things are from Him,
and we exist for Him.
And there is one Lord, Jesus Christ.
All things are through Him,
and we exist through Him.

WEEK 41

Get Over The Hump Day 2+2=TRUTH Devotional:

Every word of God proves TRUE;
He is a shield to those who take refuge in him.

PROVERBS 30:5

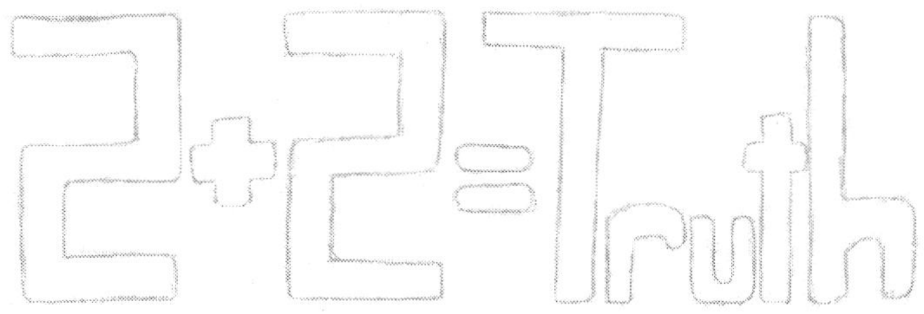

Your feelings matter, but sometimes it just doesn't matter how you feel.

So I've spent months reading blogs about different "hot button" issues, and reading so many opinions on things like homosexuality, abortion, divorce, acceptance, bullying, parenting, etc. Some people make great points, and others are just...well, ridiculous. I cannot

stress enough that each Christian should be SERIOUS about KNOWING what GOD's WORD says. Please stop relying on Sundays to "get you through the week." Christians need to be studying, reading, and praying every day for discernment. Then we can KNOW what the answers are to most of these issues today. And here's why.
2+2=4
That's right. It doesn't matter, and never will matter, how you feel about that equation. As stated above, "Your feelings matter, but it doesn't matter how you feel," because how you feel about 2+2 will never change the fact that the answer is, and always will be, 4. It doesn't matter if you have a friend or family member who believes that the answer is 5. It doesn't matter if you have this strong feeling that the answer is 6. And it will never matter that you had a pastor tell you it was 3. Because it will always and forever be 4.

The BIBLE states many truths that clearly cover these issues that are out there today (none of which I'm specifically covering here in this devotion). I'm simply pointing to The Word of God, and helping us remember that The Truth is there. It's not hiding, and it's not gonna change no matter how you, your friends, your family, or someone you respect thinks otherwise.

<u>JOHN 12:48</u>
The one who rejects me and does not receive my words has a judge; the word that I have spoken will judge him on the last day.

If you don't stand on His word, His word will Judge you and...

<u>PROVERBS 30:5-6</u>
Every word of God proves true; he is a shield to those who take refuge in him. Do not add to his words, lest he rebuke you and you be found a liar.

<u>JOHN 14:21</u>
Whoever has my commandments and keeps them, he it is who loves me. And he who loves me will be loved by my

Father, and I will love him and manifest myself to him."

There is a simple way to show you love Christ: Keep His Word. Those who disrespect it and ignore it do not love Him, no matter what they "say."

<u>2 TIMOTHY 3:16</u>

All Scripture is breathed out by God and profitable for teaching, for reproof, for correction, and for training in righteousness

<u>MATTHEW 24:35</u>

Heaven and earth will pass away, but my words will not pass away.

<u>COLOSSIANS 3:16</u>

Let the word of Christ dwell in you richly, teaching and admonishing one another in all wisdom, singing psalms and hymns and spiritual songs, with thankfulness in your hearts to God.

<u>PROVERBS 4:20-22</u>

My son, be attentive to my words; incline your ear to my sayings. Let them not escape from your sight; keep them within your heart. For they are life to those who find them, and healing to all their flesh.

<u>HEBREWS 4:12</u>

For the word of God is living and active, sharper than any two-edged sword, piercing to the division of soul and of spirit, of joints and of marrow, and discerning the thoughts and intentions of the heart.

We KNOW the answers to a lot of these issues today. Many people are just choosing to be liked instead of stand on The Word of God...and they will be judged for that. If you claim to love Jesus, keep His word. Even when it's not popular. Truth is, The Word is always gonna say what it says and it won't change:

<u>NUMBERS 23:19</u>

God is not man, that he should lie, or a son of man, that he should change his mind. Has he said, and will he not do it? Or has he spoken, and will he not fulfill it?

<u>JAMES 1:17</u>
Every good gift and every perfect gift is from above, coming down from the Father of lights with whom there is no variation or shadow due to change.

So let's start spreading the word: 2+2 still equals 4, no matter how we feel about it. And God's Word doesn't change, even if people don't like what it says. But if you Love Him, you will obey Him. ***On a side note: I was terrible at math, so I love 2+2=4 because it's simple yet true...and I didn't have to think about if a train left the station at 5pm and got to Disney World at the time Mickey Mouse opened the park, which is always 8am, how many stops did the train have to make to.......well you get the idea. I'm so glad to be out of school......

WEEK 42

Get Over The Hump Day DON'T JUDGE ME Devotional:

Judge Not, Lest Ye Be Judged. If you disagreed with me, then let me just say....don't judge me.

Many many years ago when I was just 17 years old, I went out with a friend of mine and we stole a street sign. It was the thing to do. I had seen street signs in people's rooms and even in restaurants. I figured it was just kind of a fun prank and pretty much overlooked by police. I was wrong. It just so happens that a police officer saw me and my friend with this sign, and the next thing I knew I was standing before the judge. He asked me to explain myself, and I yelled out, "Judge not, lest you be judged!" Ok, of course I didn't do that. I told the truth, and I got the privilege of paying for the sign. (I could have just ordered one, like those restaurants do.) I also was awarded probation for six months. So, clearly the judge was wrong to judge me, since the Bible says, "Judge not," right? WRONG. As christians we hear others quote that verse in order to avoid being told that what they are doing is wrong. Let's just delve into this 'judge not' thing so hopefully we can better understand its meaning.

The best interpreter of the Bible is....the Bible itself. So if you're going to quote MATTHEW 7, it's probably best to read the passage to get an idea of what is being said. We must also look at other places in the Bible that speak of judging,

and let the Bible interpret itself. Let's take a look at MATTHEW 7:1-5
"Do not judge so that you will not be judged. 2 For in the way you judge, you will be judged; and by your standard of measure, it will be measured to you.
3 Why do you look at the speck that is in your brother's eye, but do not notice the log that is in your own eye? 4 Or how can you say to your brother, 'Let me take the speck out of your eye,' and behold, the log is in your own eye?
5 You hypocrite, FIRST TAKE THE LOG OUT OF YOUR OWN EYE, and THEN YOU WILL SEE CLEARLY TO TAKE THE SPECK OUT OF YOUR BROTHER'S EYE.
(There is a time to judge your brother. That time is AFTER you have looked at your own life and repented of anything you may need to repent of first).

The idea that we should never judge comes mainly from those who enjoy doing wrong and do not want to be told that it is wrong. It rarely comes from someone who knows and actively reads the Bible. MATTHEW 18 gives believers an entire guideline on how to approach someone who is in sin. Obviously we must judge their actions in order to follow the mandate of scripture. Judgements are made by everyone, everyday. If someone cuts in line, or bullies someone, or throws a punch. If someone steals your wallet, you generally don't have a problem judging them as a thief, do you? You would call the police and the police would show up and say, "Dude, judge not." Of course that's ridiculous, and so is the claim that Christians should never judge. We can't judge other people's motives (1 CORINTHIANS 4:5), but we can most certainly judge their actions (JOHN 7:24). 1 CORINTHIANS 5 gives believers specific instructions that require judging. So we establish that there IS a time to judge.

Now, what is the purpose of judging others? TO RESTORE THEM. GALATIANS 6:1 - Brethren, even if anyone is caught in any trespass, you who are spiritual, RESTORE SUCH A ONE IN A SPIRIT OF GENTLENESS;

each one looking to yourself, so that you too will not be tempted.

Judge carefully when you should judge. As Christians we know that the world is lost and we must preach the gospel, which teaches that people must repent. If people must repent, then we must judge that their actions are sinful. The purpose, though, is so they can be saved and restored. When it comes to other believers, we must judge each other's actions in order to keep each other in check. To give each other accountability. To restore those who have fallen, with an understanding that next time it could be you who needs to be RESTORED. Judge? YES. Judge to feel self-righteous? NO. Always judge humbly with a desire to restore.

I hope you enjoyed this devotion, but if you didn't, don't judge too harshly. I might be reading your devotional book soon!

WEEK 43

Get Over The Hump Day FEAR NOT Devotional:

JOHN 14:27

PEACE I LEAVE WITH YOU; MY PEACE I GIVE TO YOU; NOT AS THE WORLD GIVES DO I GIVE TO YOU. DO NOT LET YOUR HEART BE TROUBLED, NOR LET IT BE FEARFUL.

Fear grips us. It happens all the time. We're afraid of the dark, not getting the promotion, someone leaving us, being hurt, death, public speaking, and basically everything that the future holds. Jerry Seinfeld did a routine on the poll that came out years ago stating that the greatest fear among the people of the United States was public speaking.

And death was #2! Jerry joked that, "according to that stat, people would rather be dead in the casket instead of the one up giving the eulogy." As usual, a very funny observation. Well done, Jerry. That's irrational, which of course is how the enemy wants us to behave. I have always had a wild and vivid imagination, and have struggled mentally for years over irrational fears at times. I even quit watching the news years ago, because it only leads to irrational fears. During the summer the news is going to run as many shark attack stories as they can to gain interest. Never mind the fact that you're more likely to get struck by lightning. So by the end of the summer I was afraid to take a shower because a shark might somehow be in there...because sharks are anywhere there is water, right?!?! Although I've not watched the news on TV for years, somehow I still know I'm supposed to be afraid of sharks, ebola, flying, eating, and anything and everything else in life. PANIC! That's what the enemy wants from us. Do you

know why you can't tickle yourself? It's because it's a panic response. Yep, although the person is laughing, the truth is they're panicked. Not so funny now, is it?!?! Of course it's fun to trigger other people's panic buttons. We just hate it when people mess with ours. My kids love to hide around the corner and scare us every chance they get, and I can appreciate it. I used to do the same to my brother. I still can see his feet come clean off the ground one time in our basement when I jumped out of the closet and screamed. His eyes and mouth opened real wide, and his hands did this weird thing and shot up in the air. And his feet just came right out from under him, and he landed on his behind. Priceless. However, as Christians God has given one command more times than any other in the Bible: DO NOT BE AFRAID. No matter what your fear is, IF you are HIS CHILD, He tells us:
JOHN 14:27 - Peace I leave with you; My peace I give unto you: not as the world giveth, give I unto you. LET NOT

YOUR HEART BE TROUBLED, NEITHER LET IT BE FEARFUL.

My kids and I were studying the Fruit of The Spirit (GALATIANS 5), and I started out with this verse: 2 TIMOTHY 1:7 - For God hath not given us THE SPIRIT OF FEAR, but of POWER, and of LOVE, and of A SOUND MIND.

I love that verse!!

A sound mind, not an irrational one.

Now we could go on for days, but this is a devotional, not a novel. And there are a lot of things to cover when we talk about anxiety and fear. I just want you to remember today that if you struggle with fear and anxiety, be encouraged.

Because if you're His child, He has given you THE POWER, from HIS SPIRIT, to OVERCOME YOUR FEARS by better understanding HIS LOVE FOR YOU. Don't let the enemy push you to be irrational. Use YOUR SOUND MIND to express YOUR LOVE FOR GOD as you take great joy in knowing that YOUR HEAVENLY FATHER LOVES YOU so very much.

Here are a few more verses about NOT FEARING:
ISAIAH 41:10 "So do not fear, for I am with you; do not be dismayed, for I am your God. I will strengthen you and help you; I will uphold you with my righteous right hand."
PSALM 56:3 "When I am afraid, I put my trust in you."
PHILIPPIANS 4:6-7 "Do not be anxious about anything, but in every situation, by prayer and petition, with thanksgiving, present your requests to God. And the peace of God, which transcends all understanding, will guard your hearts and your minds in Christ Jesus."
JOHN 14:27 "Peace is what I leave with you; it is my own peace that I give you. I do not give it as the world does. Do not be worried and upset; do not be afraid."
ISAIAH 43:1 "But now, this is what the Lord says…Fear not, for I have redeemed you; I have summoned you by name; you are mine."
PSALM 23:4 "Even though I walk through the valley of the shadow of death, I will fear no evil, for you are with

me; your rod and your staff, they comfort me."
JOSHUA 1:9 "Have I not commanded you? Be strong and courageous. Do not be terrified; do not be discouraged, for the Lord your God will be with you wherever you go."
ISAIAH 35:4 "Tell everyone who is discouraged, Be strong and don't be afraid! God is coming to your rescue…"
PSALM 27:1 "The Lord is my light and my salvation—whom shall I fear? The Lord is the stronghold of my life—of whom shall I be afraid?"
MARK 6:50 "Immediately he spoke to them and said, 'Take courage! It is I. Don't be afraid.'"
DEUTERONOMY 31:6 "Be strong and courageous. Do not be afraid or terrified because of them, for the Lord your God goes with you; he will never leave you nor forsake you."
ISAIAH 41:13-14 "'For I am the Lord, your God, who takes hold of your right hand and says to you, Do not fear; I will help you. Do not be afraid, for I myself

will help you,' declares the Lord, your Redeemer, the Holy One of Israel."

PSALM 118:6-7 "The Lord is with me; I will not be afraid. What can man do to me? The Lord is with me; he is my helper."

1 PETER 3:14 "But even if you suffer for doing what is right, God will reward you for it. So don't worry or be afraid of their threats."

PSALM 34:4 "I prayed to the Lord, and he answered me. He freed me from all my fears."

REVELATION 1:17 "Then he placed his right hand on me and said: 'Do not be afraid. I am the First and the Last.'"

MARK 5:36 "Jesus told him, 'Don't be afraid; just believe.'"

***Side note: If you don't know Christ, you SHOULD be afraid. There is much to fear. (MATTHEW 10:28 Jesus says - And fear not them that kill the body, but are not able to kill the soul; but rather fear Him that is able to destroy both soul and body in hell.) His FEAR NOT promises are, according to Scripture, only for His children. The good news is that He wants you to be His child. Now's a good time to begin a conversation with Jesus. Maybe just start by telling Him that you're afraid. Give Him your heart, and enjoy the feeling of all your fears falling away.)

WEEK 44

Get Over The Hump Day SELF CONTROL Devotional:

I was driving one day, and I came to a stop light next to our local Wal-Mart. The car in front of me had a bumper sticker that read: “Honk if you love Jesus.” Now I don’t normally feel compelled to show my faith by honking horns, sending on chain letters, or liking posts. However, I was feeling pretty good and was in a honking mood and felt like supporting the driver who had decided they would attract honks from others. Honk your faith, I guess. So, I honked. What happened next still makes me laugh. The little old lady driving the car gave me the finger! And no, she wasn't telling me I was number one. No, I'm not joking, and yes, that really happened. I laughed until I cried. I think I may have even pulled over, because it was becoming difficult to drive due to the fact that I was laughing so hard. The point is, that lady had forgotten what she was broadcasting and had lost control of herself for the moment. We all have those moments as believers where we don't really look like the Jesus that we claim to love and desire to emulate. We all have bad days, but our goal is to become steady, not shaken or tossed about by the circumstances in life. We see in those great ones that have gone before us the steadiness of character that we should strive to attain. Paul being content in every circumstance, John going from a man wanting to call down fire on people to being called the disciple of love. When we have The Holy Spirit living in us, I don't believe that He will ever be satisfied until we are Christ-like. So I'm calling on all of us to become more serious about our faith than we were yesterday. To become self-controlled and stop using phrases like "he makes me so mad." Because no one can "make" you angry (see Jesus when being struck and spit upon and His response for examples). You must "choose" your behavior, and own it when you fail, and ask forgiveness. We have The SPIRIT of SELF CONTROL. It has been given to all believers, and in order to use it we must understand that the power to use it comes from a DAILY walk with The Lord. Through study, prayer, and meditating on Him, The Fruit He has given us comes to life. When we're apart from the power source, we have no power....duh. Be encouraged. You already have the ability to stop those bad habits and/or sins and take control by walking with The One who

has already won the battle and given you the Spirit of Self-Control.
GALATIANS 5 (the fruit of THE SPIRIT is: love, joy, peace, patience, kindness, goodness, faithfulness, gentleness and SELF-CONTROL)
2 TIMOTHY 1:7 (God has not given us a Spirit of fear, but of love, power and SELF-CONTROL)
So if someone honks at you in traffic today...control yourself (especially your "fingers").

WEEK 45

Get Over The Hump Day BITTERNESS Devotional:

When life hands you lemons, I say throw that junk away! When my daughter was very young, I think around 4 years old, and we'd go out to eat she loved to eat lemons. It made me cringe every time, but we enjoyed watching her face as she would bite into them and make this face where her eyes would squint but her lips would kind of smile. That was so entertaining.

We'll come back to that in a moment. But I'd like to share a different story with you before I come back to the lemons.

In high school I learned to rock climb. I'll never forget the first time I went. It was in the Smoky Mountains, and it was a beautiful day. For the first time I was scaling a rock. I was Spiderman! Except Spidey seems to climb with ease, and I was nearing the top of the rock and my legs were shaking involuntarily and my forearms were in pain. I was getting tight and my fingers were slipping. I went from having fun to fearing for my life in a matter of seconds. I was in the middle of being praised by my friends for doing so well for my first time when I yelled out that I was slipping. I remember yelling, "I'm slipping, what do I do??," and the response came...."Let go!" I remember thinking how stupid that was. Let go? Yeah, ok, isn't that like saying, "Just fall to your death!" So they said it again,

"Let go, we've got you." Yeah, they had me alright. They apparently had something against me and brought me out here to die!! I no longer had a choice. My hands finally gave out and slipped off of the rock, and I fell....about a foot. Then as I hung there in the air next to the rock, I thought, "Oh, this safety equipment actually serves a purpose, huh?" and I gained my composer, got my strength back up, got back on the rock, and finished the climb.

Hopefully I can bring these two stories together to make a point as we move into the Thanksgiving season.

Let me encourage you as we move into the holiday season to do with any bitterness that you may have against family or friends what I did on that rock, and "LET GO." You can try to hang on to your bitterness, but sooner or later your body will give out on you. We aren't built to hold on to bitterness. We're designed to "Let it go," as Elsa from Frozen so beautifully sang. Did you know that arguably the most bitter substance in the world is something called denatonium and is available under the trade name Bitrex? It is the most bitter compound known. They use it as an aversion agent to prevent accidental ingestion of toxic chemicals such as antifreeze. They add this compound to help prevent people from drinking antifreeze and other dangerous substances, or as a way to prevent nail-biting. That stuff is super nasty. The point is that they use something bitter because the body automatically knows to SPIT IT OUT! Get it out of your life. It is nasty! The Bible tells us in EPHESIANS 4:31 "Let ALL BITTERNESS and wrath and anger and clamor and slander be put away from you along with all malice. Be kind to one another, tender-hearted, forgiving each other, Just as God in Christ also has forgiven you." HEBREWS 12:14-15 "Strive for peace with everyone, and for the holiness without which no one will see the Lord. See to it that no one fails to obtain the grace of God; that no "root of bitterness" springs up and causes trouble, and by it many become defiled;..."

My daughter has stopped eating lemons. It was hard for those of us watching to comprehend why someone would want to eat something so nasty and bitter/sour, but it was entertaining to watch. However, when it's someone we love constantly eating the bitterness of life it's hard to stomach and it's hard to be around. This may be you, or someone that you will see over the holidays. If it's you with the bitter heart, "Let Go." God has got you and wants something better for you. If it's someone you love with the bitter heart, love them. Share with them that God loves them. Make amends if you can. If you can't, pray for them. Maybe soon they will stop eating the lemons and you can look back and laugh. Now go buy some lemons and go rock climbing!

WEEK 46

Get Over The Hump Day WHATEVER YOU DO Devotional:

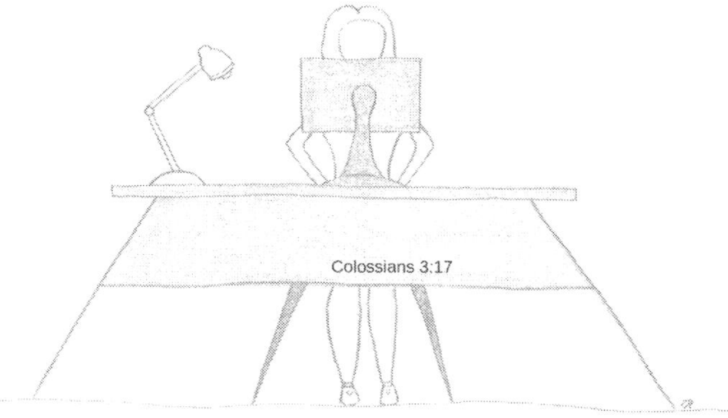

Whatever you do in word or deed, do all in the name of the Lord Jesus, giving thanks through Him to God the Father.

When I was a kid I used to go around the house and take things from my parents (finger nail clippers, pens, utensils, etc.). I would make up my bed really nice, and I would spread out all those things on my bed and put a price underneath them and have a sale. I would invite "everyone" in my family to come. That would be mom, dad, and my older brother. Then I would sell them back their stuff. I thought I was brilliant! I don't know how they did it, but it seems the government has stolen my idea!!! OK, a little joke there...LOL. When I look back now I realize of course that I was, in fact, pretty ridiculous. My parents had every right to come in and laugh at me, and then take their stuff back. But instead they chose to allow me to do something useful with their stuff. This reminds me a little of how God works. We really don't have anything that isn't already His. I think it's important to realize that we own NOTHING.

COLOSSIANS 1:15-17 says, "He (Jesus) is the image of the invisible God, the firstborn of all creation. 16 For by Him all things were created, both in the heavens and on earth, visible and invisible, whether thrones or dominions or rulers or authorities—ALL THINGS HAVE BEEN CREATED THROUGH HIM AND FOR HIM. 17 He is before all things, and in Him all things hold together.

In this life we should be taking what is His and using it to glorify Him (by Him and for Him).

Whatever you do out there for a living, it has been given to you to use for Him. I have had many different jobs, including hauling hay, and selling newspaper subscriptions. I've done a few commercials, modeled once for a pet store (I'm not kidding), worked The Jaws ride at Universal Studios, almost worked at a professional theatre in Clearwater, FL (the owner was arrested before the show ever happened...ouch), and sold clothes at Calvin Klein. I worked construction (for a very short time...lol), was a summer missionary at Hilton Head Island and Panama City Beach, waited tables on the beach and also at a catfish place (I believe everyone should have to be a server at least once in their lifetime), was a youth minister, and I was a Kids Club host for The WB before it became The CW...just to name a few. God has always been with me in my travels and through many trials at many different jobs. He has always given me a conviction to do what I do FOR HIM with ALL MY HEART. Frankly, I have failed more times than I could ever remember. But He loves me, and as long as I live, and I pray that as long as you who are reading this live, we together as brothers and sisters in Christ will realize that ALL things are His and should be used for His Glory.

So, wherever you may be reading this, let me encourage you to give thanks to Him for what you have and commit to use it for His glory.

COLOSSIANS 3:17 "AND WHATEVER YOU DO, IN WORD OR DEED, DO EVERYTHING IN THE NAME OF THE LORD JESUS, GIVING THANKS TO GOD THE FATHER THROUGH HIM.

WEEK 47

Get Over The Hump Day
GRATEFULNESS Devotional:

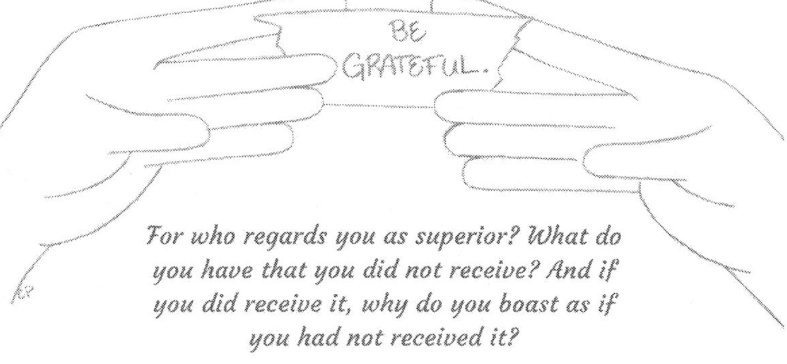

For who regards you as superior? What do you have that you did not receive? And if you did receive it, why do you boast as if you had not received it?

1 Corinthians 4:7

When I was in high school I was smitten with a cheerleader. I know...I'm the first person ever, right? She was young, blonde, and so cute! I finally got up the nerve to ask her on a date, and she said YES! Frankly, I didn't know her very well, and the reason I asked her out was simply because I thought she was attractive. (Note to all single people: This is not the appropriate reason to ask someone out. Uhm...I get that it's somewhat important, but this person will someday be someone's granny/ grandpa. I hope you get what I'm driving at here....no offense to any grannies/ gradpas out there. I'm just saying you don't normally hear people saying, "Let's go to the nursing home and check out the hot chicks or the good looking men," right?) I was so excited that someone that I found so attractive actually said they would go out with little ole me! Unfortunately, while we were on this date it seemed that SHE also found herself very attractive and therefore I found that to be extremely unattractive. She seemed to only talk about herself as the date went on and on and on and oooooonnnnn. I was so disappointed. Finally, I drove her home as quickly as possible. And as we sat in her driveway she sat staring at me waiting on a goodnight kiss. I was in a quandary. This is what I originally had foreseen and wanted, but now the fantasy had been crushed under the weight of reality. So I turned to her and gave her a big......HIGH FIVE! Yes I gave her a high five. She looked at me very confused and we never really talked again.

I've never understood why anyone would ever be "prideful" about their looks. I mean, maybe being prideful about how you have performed at some level at some skill in which you've worked really hard at least makes some sense to me. But your looks? You literally did nothing. You didn't have anything to do with the way you look. You were conceived and birthed, and you came out looking like one or both of your parents.....period. You had nothing to do with it and have no basis on which to be prideful. Yet so many people walk around proud of themselves as if they have accomplished something.....sigh. Oh well, I digress. Here's my point:

1 CORINTHIANS 4:7 (NASB) For who regards you as superior? What do you have that you did not receive? And

if you did receive it, why do you boast as if you had not received it?

We have no right to boast, but we have every right to be GRATEFUL for what we have received from the hand of Almighty God. There's nothing we have that He hasn't given us. We have received so many things from God's hand. We didn't earn it or deserve it. You may have worked hard, but God is the One who gave you that ability and that drive and that body and those hands. We own nothing, but have been given everything by the hand of GOD and therefore have "no reason to boast." So let's be grateful. Yes, let's be thankful to our God who has given us so much.

Side note: even bad things that happen are an opportunity to be Thankful. Without darkness we would never understand what light is and how it works. Without bitterness we'd never understand how sweet, sweetness really is. God's truth is ever so sweet, isn't it? THANK GOD!

WEEK 48

Get Over The Hump Day CHRISTMAS GIFTS Devotional:

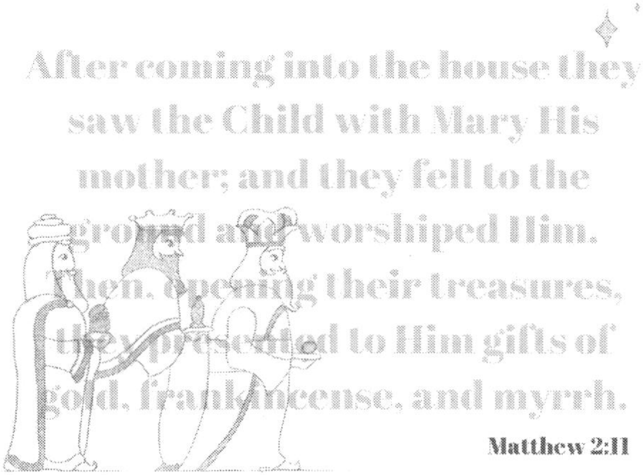

After coming into the house they saw the Child with Mary His mother; and they fell to the ground and worshiped Him. Then, opening their treasures, they presented to Him gifts of gold, frankincense, and myrrh.

Matthew 2:11

I love Christmas. I always would fall asleep with a red bell that played Christmas tunes and lit up on every note. I have no idea how anyone could ever sleep with something like that right by their bed, but I did. I also had my parents put my gifts under a blanket so I could feel for them and pull them out one by one and open them. Yeah, I'm strange. But that probably shouldn't surprise anyone by now. Many of us remember our favorite Christmas gifts: the bike, the easy-bake oven, the red rider bb gun, the video gaming system, the jewelry, the Tickle-me Elmo, the engagement ring. Gifts are wonderful expressions of our love for each other. My brother and I usually came up with some gag gift. For example, one year it wasn't really the gift but the wrapping paper. He was jobless, so I wrapped all his gifts in the classified ads and highlighted the jobs I thought fit him. Then there was the year he gave me 50 gift cards to a bunch of different places, and I had to find the two that actually had money on them. The point is that gifts mean something.

The gift of God's Son should be that one gift that is thought of every day and that is never taken for granted or forgotten. And the gifts He was given at His birth had meaning as well.

MATTHEW 2:11- On coming to the house, they saw the child with his mother Mary, and they bowed down and worshiped Him. Then they opened their treasures and presented Him with gifts of gold and of incense and of myrrh.

Gold was associated with kings, and Christians believe that Jesus is the King of Kings.

Frankincense was a perfume used in Jewish worship and, as a gift, it showed that people would worship Jesus.

Myrrh was a perfume that was put on dead bodies to make them smell nice and, as a gift, it showed that Jesus would suffer and die for our sins.

I just want to prepare for this season by reminding myself and all who read this that our Lord came for a reason. The gifts given had a purpose to them (Gold: He is our King, Frankincense: He is worthy of our worship, Myrrh: He died for our sins and conquered death, hell, and the grave). And we also have a purpose. We're here to bring glory to God with the gifts we've been given. Maybe you're a great encourager, or great with giving of your time. Maybe you are really good at listening or writing cards or making others laugh. Maybe you have the gift of being patient, which comes in real handy at the family dinners. Remember that this Christmas. You have been given a gift. That gift has a purpose. (1 CORINTHIANS 10:31 So, whether you eat or drink, or whatever you do, do all to the glory of God.) (COLOSSIANS 3:17 And whatever you do, in word or deed, do everything in the name of the Lord Jesus, giving thanks to God the Father through him.) Use your gifts for His glory and the good of others. Now go forth and be a cheerful giver!

WEEK 49

Get Over The Hump Day BLOOD AT THE MANGER Devotional:

I remember one year in our youth group we were running short on boys. That's a difficult position to be in when you're trying to put on a Christmas pageant with shepherds and wise men. So we just took some of the girls with long hair, pulled it under their chins, and put a rubber band in it to make it look like they had beards. Ya gotta work with what you got, ya know? People there understood, and it worked just fine. It was kind of funny, though. We walked through the motions and stood in our places as people sang the traditional Christmas songs. It was....nice.

Now fast forward to last year as I'm reading my kids (3rd and 5th graders at that time) the Christmas story from The Bible. As I'm reading Scripture I like to try to explain to my kids what's going on. And that's when it hit me. The manger scene was nothing like we portray it in our church pageants. Those are nice, and they serve a great purpose of remembering the story. However, those pageants, as great as they are, don't really tell the actual story, do they? We like to create a pretty comfortable scene at the end where Mary and Joseph are standing there in robes holding a baby doll and you've got the shepherds on one side and the 3 wise men on the other side.

The only problem is that it was not a pretty scene at all in that manger. To my knowledge barns are not clean. They are filled with slop and poop. They smell pretty bad, depending on what animals you have in there. But all of those animals poop, so it pretty much is going to smell. I was there both times when my children were born, and let me tell you, there was a lot of screaming and pushing and pain in that room...and that was all just me! Imagine what my wife was going through! Seriously, there was blood at the manger. There was poop at the manger. There was a placenta. And there were two very young parents at the manger with no doctors or epidurals. The witnesses to this would have been dirty, smelly, rough shepherds who had been recently scared nearly to death by angels and told to drop by and see the most important sight they would ever see. God Himself placed in a feeding trough. Real gritty stuff. That's the way God chose to send His Son into this world.

That is the very definition of HUMILITY. Royalty placed in a trough, by choice.

I'm not gonna boycott Christmas pageants, and I'm not gonna rain on your gift-giving or tell you how and what you should or shouldn't say about Santa. I've got my own theories about that guy, lol. What I am gonna do is teach people the truth about what went down that night. Because later in life when things get difficult, and they will, maybe someone will remember that this life never has been about our own comfort. If it wasn't about His comfort, it certainly isn't about ours. Life is about the salvation that came that night and how much we should bow low to this humble King that would do this for us. How can we glorify Him? How can we show our thanks for doing what He has done for us? How many people can we share this with so they'll understand what this life is about? We're surrounded by a culture determined to be comfortable, and they will try to make the Bible say what they want it to say to fit their lifestyle choices. But lies and money and connections won't save us when that little baby boy comes back. This time it won't be in helpless fashion. It will be in unstoppable, unexplainable, undeniable wrath and power. That little baby grew up and defeated death, hell, and the grave. He is now The Mighty Warrior and The King of Kings, and He demands your attention and your worship. I'm gonna give it to Him. I hope you do too. The alternative will not be....well, comfortable. Merry Real Gritty Christmas to you all!

LUKE 2 In those days a decree
went out from Caesar Augustus that all
the world should be registered. 2 This
was the first registration when Quirinius
was governor of Syria. 3 And all went to
be registered, each to his own town.
4 And Joseph also went up from Galilee,
from the town of Nazareth, to Judea, to
the city of David, which is called
Bethlehem, because he was of the
house and lineage of David, 5 to be
registered with Mary, his betrothed, who
was with child. 6 And while they were
there, the time came for her to give

birth. 7 And she gave birth to her
firstborn son and wrapped him in
swaddling cloths and LAID HIM IN A
MANGER, BECAUSE THERE WAS NO
PLACE FOR THEM IN THE INN.
8 And in the same region there were
shepherds out in the field, keeping
watch over their flock by night. 9 And an
angel of the Lord appeared to them, and
the glory of the Lord shone around
them, and they were filled with great
fear. 10 And the angel said to them,
"Fear not, for behold, I bring you good
news of great joy that will be for all the
people. 11 For unto you is born this day
in the city of David a Savior, who is
Christ the Lord. 12 And this will be a
sign for you: you will find a baby
wrapped in swaddling cloths and LYING
IN A MANGER."

2 PETER 3:10-13 But the day of the Lord will come like a thief. On that day the heavens will pass away with a dreadful noise, the elements will be consumed by fire, and the earth and all the works done on it will be exposed.

11 Since everything will be destroyed in
this way, what sort of people ought you
to be? You must live holy and godly
lives, 12 waiting for and hastening the
coming day of God. Because of that
day, the heavens will be destroyed by
fire and the elements will melt away in
the flames. 13 But according to his
promise we are waiting for a new
heaven and a new earth, where
righteousness is at home.

WEEK 50

Get Over The Hump Day MENDING WHAT'S BROKEN Devotional:

Have you ever been Broken on Christmas?

Bean and Bailey had a show during the Christmas season and I was doing my impersonation of Michael Jackson (If you haven't seen this, feel free to check it out at our website: www.beanandbailey.com). And in the middle of doing the moonwalk, my toe

did something that hurt really badly. It felt like it popped out of place. I thought it might possibly be broken. I just knew my friends would have fun with that one.
Friend: "Hey man, how'd you break your toe?"
Me: "Doing the moonwalk"
Friend: "No seriously, how'd you break your toe?"

And you can imagine the rest. So I went to see the orthopedic surgeon, who took an X-Ray and told me I had turf toe...and that it would probably take about 6 months to a year to fully heal. And then she squeezed my foot in a different place and asked if it hurt where she had squeezed. I said, "uhm, no." Then she said, "That's funny, because there's a small fracture there." I asked what we needed to do about it. She said "nothing," and I went home. My toe got better, and I never knew about the other injury. But I've never had any problems with it.

The crazy thing is, I was broken and didn't even know it. It wasn't until something else "bad" happened that my

eyes were opened to something else that was wrong. We hear the question at times, "Why do bad things happen to good people?" Well, truth is, there are no "good" people. Only a "good" God. (MATTHEW 19:16-17 Now behold, one came and said to Him, "Good Teacher, what good thing shall I do that I may have eternal life?"
17 So He said to him, "Why do you call Me good? No one is good but One, that is, God.....) Soooo, the only thing that can make someone good at all is God living in you. Bad things happen because we live in a world full of sin, and it will be that way until He comes back. Not to mention, without bad we wouldn't understand what is good. Unless you've experienced darkness you can't appreciate light. Without ugliness, we don't appreciate beauty. Unless something is broken, we don't know it needs to be fixed. It could be that "bad" thing that happens to you is actually a "good" thing in disguise, designed to show you that you are broken so you can let God fix what

needs to be mended in your life. Are you broken? The good thing about being broken is that at least you know you need to be fixed. The scary thing is those souls who are broken and don't know it. The Bible teaches us that we are ALL broken. (ROMANS 3:23 - For ALL have sinned and fallen short of the Glory of God). The good news is that you and anyone you know can be fixed. (ROMANS 10:9 - If you confess with your mouth that Jesus is Lord and believe in your heart that God raised him from the dead, you will be saved.)

I think the greatest Christmas gift you can give this year is the The Truth. Let's give that out to our family and friends this year with love. Let's be about mending the broken hearted. That sure seems like CHRISTmas to me.

WEEK 51

Get Over The Hump Day CHRISTMAS EVE Devotional:

(The In-Laws are Coming....everyone hide!)

At Christmas time at my grandparents' house (or the in-laws or others homes), I was always concerned that my reaction wouldn't be good enough when I opened a gift. You know,

I typically feel more excited than I show, but that's not a great personality trait when someone is giving you a gift and watching you open it. Therefore, I began trying to match my facial expressions with my inner excitement. Of course there was also the one year that I had trouble not laughing when my grandmother gave my brother and I matching fuzzy steering wheel covers. It's hard when the gift is hilarious and you're not sure if they were trying to be funny or not. She, in that case, was not. I still have that fuzzy steering wheel cover, and I still laugh every time I look at it or think about that Christmas.

My nephew Max, before he was really old enough to understand that there were gifts inside the wrapped boxes, tore off the wrapping paper one Christmas and yelled, "Look! A BOX!!" He was pumped. He was almost confused to find out he wasn't done opening the gift. That was great. I wish it was always like that when we opened gifts.

There will always be good gifts, bad gifts, funny gifts, etc., and it seems we will forever be trying to make sure we're acting proper so as not to hurt anyone's feelings (and then re-gifting that candle at the office Christmas party). There is one gift that should forever be given and received and re-gifted over and over again. And that is the gift of God's love. Here is a passage of scripture I want us to think about this Christmas, and one part of it specifically.

1 CORINTHIANS 13:4-7 Love is patient and kind; love does not envy or boast; it is not arrogant or rude. It does not insist on its own way; it is not irritable or resentful; it does not rejoice at wrongdoing, but rejoices with the truth. Love bears all things, believes all things, hopes all things, endures all things.

Each one of these points deserves a lesson of its own, but this Christmas when we're loving those that are hard to love (maybe even in our own families as we're forced to see them during this holiday season!! LOL) let's focus on the one little section of that verse that says: LOVE DOES NOT INSIST ON IT'S OWN WAY. I don't care how you've done it for the last 25 years, or how many years in a row you've opened what gifts in what order, or eaten what food at what time. Let's attempt to see beyond ourselves and how we think it SHOULD all go, and understand that everyone is on a path...and our job is to love them in a way that enlightens that path. We can't push them onto another path or yank them off course by demanding they do things our way. We can model the verse above and trust that God can shine a light through our obedience. He's really good at taking people's obedience and making it shine. His Son comes to mind. He was obedient to the point of death, and, because of that, I now have life. By the way, you can have that light in your own life too. But to obtain it you must let go of insisting on your own way. You must come through faith in The Lord Jesus Christ (EPHESIANS 2:8-9). Let's try things His way. I'm pretty sure we'll see a big difference if we do. We might not even have to tell people that this season is about Jesus. They might just know it by the way we love them. Let's get outside our little box this year and get excited about loving people...even if it is your in-laws.

I hope you have a Merry Christmas!!!

WEEK 52

Get Over The Hump Day A NEW PERSPECTIVE Devotional:

It's New Years Eve. It's time for a new perspective!

My cousin Darby and I, when we were about 5 years old, were at my grandmother's house. All the adults were downstairs playing Rook (their tradition). We were the only kids there, and we were upstairs watching Dick Clark drop the ball in NYC. And we decided to do something different. We did headstands and stood on our heads for the entire last minute while they dropped the ball. We haven't missed a year since. We've done that every year for the past 30 something years. We've stood on our heads for the last minute in AL,AR,CA,CT,FL,GA,HI,IN,KY,KS,MA, MD,MI,MN,MO,MS,NC,NY,OH,OK,PA,R I,SC,TN,VA,WV and our nation's capital, good old Washington DC. Each one of them all have their own story. Each year is new and unique. And so are you, if you are in Christ.

2 CORINTHIANS 5:16-17 -From now on, therefore, WE REGARD NO ONE ACCORDING TO THE FLESH. Even though we once regarded Christ according to the flesh, we regard him thus no longer. Therefore, IF ANYONE IS IN CHRIST, HE IS A NEW CREATION. The old has passed away; behold, the new has come.

If you are a Christian, remember that you are a NEW CREATION and therefore you should be training yourself to have a new perspective. You should see things differently from the world. Love is different to you. It's not a feeling; it's a person. It's Christ Himself (1JOHN 4:8). There are spiritual attributes that should be flowing from you that are fruit of THE SPIRIT that is IN YOU (GALATIANS 5:22-23): Love, Joy, Peace, Patience, Kindness, Goodness, Faithfulness, Gentleness and Self-Control. You must train yourself with the help of The Holy Spirit to see this life differently. You are not perfect, but that is your goal (MATTHEW 5:48 Ye therefore shall be perfect, as your heavenly Father is perfect). It's a goal you can't attain while here on earth. But you run after it because you want to be like Christ and to drink in His love and to feel what it's like to be wonderfully different. You will begin to see people in a different way. Instead of seeing an attractive woman, you will begin to see a spiritual person who may need prayer. Or instead of that co-worker that annoys you to death, you will begin to see someone who lacks confidence and needs encouragement. Paul says that as believers “we regard no one according to the flesh.” It’s time to train our eyes and ears to see and hear from a new spiritual perspective. The year is new and so are you, so let’s seize this new opportunity.

Happy New....You.

Acknowledgments:

Thank you GOD for the idea to write this devotional! I've learned so much and grown closer to YOU in the process! I guess I need to acknowledge Google for helping me find scriptures quickly as well as sites like BibleGateway.com and GotQuestions.org for great reference help. The illustrations were done by my daughter Ella Bailey and Caitlin Pearson (one of our "daughters from another mother", is that how the saying goes?) I'd like to acknowledge my wife, Kimberly, my daughter, Ella, and my son, Dean, for being awesome and for being an inspiration to me every day. I'd like to acknowledge my friend, and partner in crime, Bradley Bean, who helped me edit this book even though I kept some of the "incorrect punctuation" in place on purpose because I just like to drive people crazy that way.....LOL! Thanks to Tim Hawkins for the kind words. Finally, Tisha Wright, thank you so much for helping me organize this project, and for teaching me how to edit, paste, copy, and basically use the internet. God Bless You All! Thanks also to anyone who reads this, I hope it helps you get over that hump!

Thanks,
Jackson Bailey